NEW WORKS IN ACCOUNTING HISTORY

Richard P. Brief, *Series Editor*

Leonard N. Stern School of Business
New York University

A Garland Series

FINANCIAL REPORTING FOR NONPROFIT ORGANIZATIONS

A Fresh Look

Robert K. Mautz

Garland Publishing, Inc.
New York and London 1994

Library of Congress Cataloging-in-Publication Data

Mautz, R.K. (Robert Kuhn), 1915–

   Financial reporting for nonprofit organizations: a fresh look / Robert
K. Mautz.
      p. cm. — (New works in accounting history)
   Includes bibliographical references and index.
   ISBN-0-8153-1718-2 (acid-free paper)
   1. Nonprofit organizations—United States—Accounting. 2. Financial
statements—United States. 3. Accounting—United States—History. I.
Title. II. Series.
HF5686.N56M38   1994   93–40062
657'.98—dc20   CIP

All volumes printed on acid-free, 250-year-life paper.
Manufactured in the United States of America.

Design by Marisel Tavarez

FOR
WILFORD G. EDLING

CONTENTS

PREFACE

Few accountants, and fewer non-accountants, show much
interest in the financial statements of not-for-profit organizations. Why is this so? Not-for-profit organizations touch our
lives in many ways. Most adult Americans, for example, have
direct relationships as contributors, beneficiaries, or both, with
several such organizations. We probably pay taxes to two or
three; we contribute to a church and to any number of eleemo-
synary organizations like the Red Cross and the United Way;
we also help support medical research and ecological organizations; and we belong to one or more social, fraternal, and
professional groups. As we age, we tend to find ourselves in
condominiums where we belong to a home owners association. For many of us, a substantial part of our personal income
goes to not-for-profit organizations. Why then do we have so
little interest in their financial statements?

Consider the following questions:

In how many nonprofit organizations do you have an
interest, either as a contributor, a beneficiary, or both?

When did you last study, or even carefully read, a set of
financial statements for a nonprofit organization?

Were the statements prepared in accordance with
generally accepted accounting principles?

How much of the reported information did you find
understandable and useful for your purpose, whatever
that purpose may have been?

The reason for such a lack of interest is found in the likely
responses to the last two questions above. At the present time,
the reports of most publicly reporting nonprofit organizations
are prepared, at least allegedly, in accordance with generally

accepted accounting principles. Therein lies the fault. Generally accepted accounting principles have been developed over considerable time and at great cost to be responsive to the needs of those who have an interest in the success of forprofit business organizations. Thoughtful analysis shows business organizations and nonprofit organizations differ greatly in respects that should influence their accounting and financial reporting.

Applying generally accepted accounting principles for business organizations to not-for-profit entities sometimes results in mystifying and nearly incomprehensible financial reporting. In this small volume, I attempt to take a fresh look at how the purposes and results of the financial activities of nonprofit organizations might better be reported.

RKM

FINANCIAL REPORTING FOR NONPROFIT ORGANIZATIONS

A Fresh Look

CHAPTER 1
A NOT-FOR-PROFIT ASSIGNMENT

A reading of the Financial Accounting Standards Board's Discussion Memorandum, *Financial Reporting by Not-for-Profit Organizations: Form and Content of Financial Statements* (August 29, 1989), leaves one with the feeling that financial reporting for not-for-profit organizations is something other than a model of clarity and precision. Some part of this may result from the impressive variety of organizations that constitute the population of not-for-profit organizations.

The characteristics that distinguish this kind of organization are "(a) contributions of significant amounts of resources from resource providers who do not expect commensurate or proportionate pecuniary return, (b) operating purposes other than to provide goods or services at a profit, and (c) absence of ownership interests like those of business enterprises." Note that these identifying characteristics are all stated in the negative. They describe features that not-for-profits do not have. This is a little like describing a group of people who do not have red hair, do something other than accounting, and are not home owners. What positive features make these people (or organizations) similar enough to constitute a classification is not clear. One result of this kind of "definition" is to permit the inclusion of items that share differences but not many similarities.

Thus we should not be surprised when the variety of organizations included as meeting the stated requirements is both varied and impressive: "cemetery organizations, civic organizations, colleges and universities, cultural institutions, fraternal organizations, hospitals, libraries, museums, nursing homes, performing arts organizations, political parties, private and community foundations, private elementary and secondary schools, professional associations, public broadcasting stations, religious organizations, research and scientific organizations, social and country clubs, trade associations, voluntary health and welfare organizations, and zoological and botanical societies."

The Discussion Memorandum specifically excludes "employee benefit and pension plans, not-for-profit entities operating essentially as commercial businesses for the direct economic benefit of members or stockholders (for example, mutual insurance companies, mutual banks, trusts, and farm cooperatives), or state and local governments and governmental units." What excludes these organizations is as unclear as what includes those that remain in the not-for-profit category.

Over the last dozen years, a number of items in the professional literature have suggested that conceptual differences between forprofits and nonprofits might call for an approach to financial reporting for nonprofits substantively different from financial reporting for forprofits. Responses to these suggestions have been minimal. Yet the mere recitation of the characteristics of nonprofit organizations cited in the Discussion Memorandum might cause the reader well grounded in the theory of income determination to pause and reflect on the importance of those chacteristics.

Given such significant conceptual differences between forprofits and nonprofits, how much, if any, conventional accounting theory and practice applies to nonprofits? My reading of the Discussion Memorandum gives me little assurance that such a question has been fully explored.

An Intellectual Exercise

One way to undertake such an exploration might be to engage in a small intellectual exercise. Let us assume we have been engaged as consultants to a large country that is changing from a tightly planned and controlled society to an open market economy. Its leaders see a role for both business organizations and nonprofit entities, and request that our firm recommend appropriate accounting and reporting for each of these. We are assigned to the nonprofit team although we have had little direct experience with nonprofit organizations and no experience in the client country. Any distinction between forprofit and nonprofit entities is to be made on conceptual grounds only; unless conceptual differences exist between organizations, the accounting and reporting should be the same for both. Nonprofit entities are estimated to provide 30% of the nation's future economic activity.

We begin our study, of course, with an attempt to discover all we can about our subjects. We learn the following:

1. The chartering and regulation of nonprofits is to be very loose. There is no intent to discourage their use. This means there may be great differences and little uniformity among not-for-profit organizations.

2. Other than illegal activities, there is almost no limitation on the scope or nature of a nonprofit's activities. Almost anyone can obtain a nonprofit charter for any legal activity.

3.   Among the interesting possibilities is that nonprofits may engage in profit-making activities as a source of funds for their nonprofit purposes.

A Classification of Nonprofit Organizations

The following classification of probable nonprofit organizations was prepared by a fellow team member:

A. Organizations that solicit funds for a stated purpose:

1. and actually spend almost all of the amounts received directly or indirectly for the purpose or purposes stated in their solicitation activities. Included might be:
Media ministries,
Traditional churches,
Medical and other research organizations,
Organizations with special or general ecological goals, and
Organizations to meet any one or more of a wide variety of human and non-human needs.

2. yet spend so little of the amounts received for the stated purpose that one must question what the organization's real purpose is.

B. Self-help organizations. These include professional organizations, condominium homeowners' associations, political parties, and many social and recreational organizations. The members work together to accomplish a joint goal or goals, and share the costs.

C. Governmental organizations. These are self-help organizations granted special powers that put them in a class by themselves. One of these powers is the ability to levy and collect taxes. Another is to effect direct transfers of wealth from taxpayers to others through "transfer payments" and/or by providing services to some people paid for with tax revenues obtained from others.

D. Break-even businesses. Public bodies and others may establish and support hospitals, utilities, and other service activities primarily to provide a public service with no expectation of profit. Nevertheless, managements of these activities are expected to operate on a business-like basis, and to hold losses to a minimum. Precisely break-even operation becomes a theoretical goal seldom attained. An occasional profit, or even a regular one, if not too large, would seldom be cause for serious criticism of management.

E. Organizations that combine nonprofit and forprofit activities. Forprofit activities are not forbidden to nonprofit organizations. Thus nonprofits may own other entities that are engaged in profit-seeking activities. They may also undertake activities directly for the purpose of raising funds. For example, a membership nonprofit organization may sell its membership list to other entities for advertising or solicitation purposes.

Some Preliminary Issues

A number of questions were posed by members of the team as they discussed the information thus far obtained. They found the classification of nonprofit organizations focused their attention on the following issues:

1. How should we think of nonprofits? As all of the above or only some of them?

2. What do we do with the profit-directed activities of nonprofit organizations? Don't these activities belong to the forprofit team?

3. Are solicitation organizations fundamentally different from organizations that obtain resources through the imposition of taxes?

4. When we talk about public reporting by nonprofit organizations, what do we have in mind? To whom will these reports be directed? What are their interests? Will the reports look like traditional financial statements?

After extensive discussion and some disagreement, the team members first decided they had to reach at least tentative conclusions on these matters in order to proceed. Because they were exploring a new subject, they could always abandon lines of exploration that proved fruitless and then try other options. With this policy established, they took up the scope of their assignment.

Essential Nature of a Nonprofit

To their surprise, they soon learned that a positive definition of nonprofits was very difficult. Criticizing the Discussion Memorandum approach was much easier than finding a better one. The vocal majority of the team finally decided that, conceptually, what distinguishes true nonprofits is the nature of their activity and their purpose. They then developed the following definition and proposed to proceed with their assignment, relying on this definition. *A true not-for-profit organization's primary emphasis is on service to meet needs; it obtains resources where it can and uses those resources to provide a service or services to recipients at no cost or at less than cost.*

But a hitherto quiet member of the team raised some questions. "When you shift your emphasis from profit to activity and purpose, don't you lose more than you gain? Isn't every business organization in the country focused on service? When I was with one of the major CPA firms, we were told constantly to be 'client service oriented,' that we were a 'full service firm,' and that whatever we were doing for a client, we should be looking for other opportunities to provide needed service. How can we exclude all profit-making organizations on the basis that they are not service oriented?"

Destroying the majority's satisfaction with its definition did not make him the most popular member of the team although it did earn him some respect. It also put a damper on the team's effort to identify and define those organizations for which it was responsible. Seeing little likelihood of more progress that day, the team leader dismissed the team members suggesting that they all give some thought to discovering a satisfactory way to proceed. After all, if not-for-profits could be defined only with a long and seemingly arbitrary list of organizations included, real progress was unlikely.

The next morning, another member of the team had a proposal. He suggested that from a financial point of view, all organizations engaging in business transactions can be divided into four groups based on the activities in which they are engaged:

1. Activities intended to increase the wealth of the owners of the organization.
2. Activities intended to transfer value from one or more persons to one or more other persons, none of which are owners of the organization.
3. Activities intended to share the costs of achieving a common goal or goals among a number of people.
4. Combinations of (1), (2) and (3).

In his explanation of this classification, the team member described business corporations as engaged in the activities described falling within Group 1. So might the activities of some nominal not-for-profits that were actually for-profits in disguise. Charitable organizations transfer value from contributors to those in need. Professional associations, political parties, condominium owners' associations, and many other organizations share the costs of seeking their objectives. Many organizations engage in activities that could include them in more than one group. For example, museums operate gift shops and publish magazines; professional organizations might engage in training programs at fees intended to augment the resources available to their members; institutions of higher learning charge tuition to most students but offer scholarships to others. Most governments are both cost sharers and value transferors.

What distinguishes not-for-profits from others is the relative proportions of their activities. An organization primarily engaged in Group 1 activities is a for-profit organization; an organization engaged primarily in cost-sharing, value transfer, or a combination of these is a not-for-profit. So the team should be concerned only with organizations whose major actvities are either cost sharing, value transfer, or a combination of these.

Wealth-Increasing Activities Conducted by Nonprofit Organizations

This led to a discussion of whether financial reporting should be based on an organization's major activity or should vary with each activity. In other words, if an organization's activities were 60 percent concerned with charitable activities (transfering values) and 40 percent involved in profit-making activities to raise additional funds for its charitable purposes, how should it report? At this point, the team leader suggested that as the team had not yet concluded how expense-sharing and value-transfer should be reported, any attempt to resolve the question would be premature. Certainly the team must face the question at some time before it completed its assignment, but that time had not yet arrived.

The team did conclude that all profit-directed (wealth-increasing) activities, no matter the primary activity of the organization involved, should be accounted for and reported under the same set of financial reporting standards. The reasoning ran something like this: all profit-directed activities share the same goal--profit. To allocate resources among such activities in an intelligent way requires the ability to compare the success of such activities on the basis of relevant information prepared on a uniform and consistent basis. Establishing standards to accomplish this was the assignment of the other team. Hence the not-for-profit entities team would inform the business entities team of this decision and await the conclusions of the business entities team.

Once these conclusions were available, the not-for-profit entities team would adopt them for determining the results of all business activities conducted by nonprofit organizations. The results of business activities, determined in compliance with business accounting standards, would then be included among the cost-sharing/value-transferring entities' sources of funds just as if those results had been contributed to share in costs or to support value transfers. However, because these are not actually the result of solicitation activities but are obtained by a different kind of effort, it appears desirable that they should be identified separately rather than lost in a single total of resources obtained.

Are Contribution and Taxing Organizations Fundamentally Similar?

The issue of whether contributions are fundamentally different from tax receipts was resolved when the team evolved this line of reasoning. Both sources provide resources to be used for the organization's purposes. Receipts from either source could be restricted to specific uses or be available for unrestricted exenditure. The terms of a tax act could limit the government's uses of the resources obtained under the act, but so could a given contributor restrict the recipient entity's use of donated funds. The solicitation efforts required to obtain contributions are not all that different from the task a city's or state's management faces in convincing citizens to accept a new or increased tax. In each case, the task is to convince the provider that the resources are needed for a worthy purpose and will not be wasted.

Finally, the argument that contributed funds and tax receipts are much more similar to one another than either is to business revenue convinced even the most skeptical.

For Whom Are Cost-Sharing/Value-Transferring Entity Reports to be Prepared?

Determining for whom published reports are to be prepared was a more difficult problem to resolve. First, organization management was eliminated as the primary user on the grounds that management was an "inside interest" that could always obtain whatever accounting information it desired and in whatever form. Published information must be for someone else. Yes, but for whom? If there is no equity interest, what other interest has either a need or a right to any information?

One of the more philosophically directed members of the team suggested that when any organization tried to obtain funds from people, those people were not likely to give up their personal resources unless the organization could give a good explanation of why it needed the funds and how they would be used. Having obtained the funds, whether through taxation or donation, it then had an obligation not only to use them for the purpose stated but to report that use to those from whom the funds were obtained. Thus there was a "closing of the loop." "We asked you for your financial support and said we would use what you gave us for this specific purpose or purposes. You gave us the resources. We used them for the stated purposes. And here is a report that tells you that we did so." This reasoning appealed to most members of the team. They agreed that their consideration of public financial reporting for nonprofit entities should emphasize the needs and interests of contributors and taxpayers as the primary users of such reports.

One of the auditors in the group added the thought that this was a great argument for requiring any published reports to be audited. Unless they have credibility, they won't serve their purpose very well.

A Dissenting View

Another member of the team had quite a different point of view. "That's all very good, but why would a contributor or a taxpayer want such information? Once the donation is made or the tax paid, it's gone. A contributor or taxpayer is not like an investor. He can't get his money back by selling his shares if he doesn't like what the the management does. It's easy to understand why shareholders are interested in the financial statements of the companies in which they own shares. They must be alert to the need to protect their investments. Shareholders continually make those old buy-hold-sell decisions. But what choices does a contributor to the United Way or a taxpayer have? Once he pays, its all over with."

"Not at all" came a response from the philosopher type. "There is always next year. He continually faces the choice of whether to donate again or not."

"Yeah, but what about taxes? There's no choice there. You know that old line about death and taxes."

"Now wait a minute. We want these people to know what their leaders are doing with that tax money. Taxpayers have a vote; they elect the management. If this is ever to be a democracy, let's help get them off on the right foot. I have a strong feeling that if our own government provided all taxpayers with an understandable accounting of how they used that money --and whether we were paying our way each year or running deeper in debt--we might take more interest in elections. If we knew what our financial interests really are and voted them, we wouldn't leave such a mess of debt to our kids."

"Well, that does make some sense. But I'm not sure that many contributors or taxpayers have that much interest. Yes, I know they should, but my experience doesn't tell me they will. And I can already hear your next argument. 'We should at least give them the chance.' That's fair enough. But now we have another problem. What kind of information should they have?"

The Focus of Nonprofit Entity Reporting
The ensuing discussion wandered over a variety of subjects such as the understandability of the FASB's cash flow statements; the preparation of a balance sheet for a service organization in which, by definition, there is no equity interest; and whether there was such a thing as a "non-income statement." Finally, one of the less vocal members of the team suggested that what most taxpayers and contributors really wanted to know about

organizations to which they made contributions or paid taxes was something like this:

How much did they get this year and from what sources?
What did they do with it?
How much do they have left?
What are their plans for next year? How much more will they want and how do they expect to get it?

The simplicity and realism of the proposal stopped the conversation for a bit. Until someone exploded with: "This isn't even accounting! All you would need is a few schedules. No operating statement, no balance sheet, no real accounting!" And then, almost as an afterthought, "But it does make some sense, doesn't it?"

Before we leave our team members temporarily, we would make a mistake not to listen to another member of the nonprofit entities team raise an issue that has long troubled him. As his explanation was drawn out a little at a time and over several days, I will take the liberty of summarizing it as follows, putting it in the first person to retain some of the flavor.

Cash-Consumers and Cash-Providers

"I have this problem that I can't seem to reconcile. We live in a city that has a good bus system. I know it's good because my Uncle Ben is the manager. The buses are clean, run on time, have good schedules, but are seldom more than half full. Morning and evening traffic in our town consists of hoards of one-person automobiles. Americans love their cars. Of course we have the traffic and pollution problems of most cities our size. The bus company advertises, the Mayor pleads, but everyone wants to drive his or her own car. So, of course the bus company operates at a loss. But it is owned by the city and gets a government subsidy.

"From every point of view, the bus system is an asset to the city. Many workers would be greatly inconvenienced without it. The city needs it. But it does cost the city to keep it going. Every year at budget time my poor old uncle suffers. The Mayor and some of the councilmen look at the size of the subsidy and seriously consider the possibility of selling the bus company. Of course, they know no one in his right mind would buy it. There is no way to run it at a profit. They even talk about selling the buses and closing down the system. But they always conclude the discussion by deciding the city needs the system and politically it would be disastrous to close it down. My uncle has only a few years to go until retirement, so we think he will make it all right. That isn't my problem.

"What bothers me is definitions. Lately, the mayor has found a term he uses a lot. He describes the bus company as a 'cash-consumer not a cash-provider.' When I read the FASB stuff, I learn that an asset is supposed to cause a net cash inflow to the company that owns it. The bus system doesn't do that. I suppose if the city were run for profit, someone would take a look at the bus company and decide it was a loser. I don't know how anyone in a business could justify keeping it in operation when it produces a loss every year. So how can it be an asset? The city values the buses and other equipment at cost less depreciation and includes them with other assets in its balance sheet. But how can the bus system be an asset if it produces a net cash outflow rather than a net cash inflow? You guys may think I'm crazy but this bugs me. Is it an asset or isn't it? What about the city parks? They are cash consumers too. Is there something about nonprofit organizations that makes our accepted accounting definitions not work very well?"

Responses of the other team members varied. Most knew this was a problem they would have to face sooner or later. One member expressed this view: "We certainly don't want to invent some new system of accounting. Nonprofit organizations can't be all that different!"

NOTES

1. "Financial Reporting: Should Government Emulate Business?", *Journal of Accountancy*, August 1981; "Monuments, Mistakes, and Opportunities," *Accounting Horizons*, June 1988; "Not-for-Profit Financial Reporting: Another View," *Journal of Accountancy*, August 1989; "Why Not-for-Profits Should Report Their Commitments,"*Journal of Accountancy*, June 1990; "Generally Accepted Accounting Principles and Federal Financial Reporting, " *Public Budgeting and Finance*, Winter 1991; all by R.K. Mautz.

CHAPTER 2
CURRENT PRACTICE
IN FINANCIAL REPORTING
FOR NONPROFIT ENTITIES

Having encouraged his team to take a "fresh look" at nonprofit organizations, the team leader thought it well to acquaint the members with some current practice in financial reporting for such organizations. For this purpose he had obtained copies of recent financial statements for three not-for-profit entities: the American Accounting Association, the American Association of Retired Persons, and the State of Utah. Because some of the exhibits in the annual reports of these entities are not legible when reproduced on the page size of this book, we will be able to "see" them only through the eyes of our consulting team. However, all of them are published, are readily available, and can easily be obtained free of charge from the entities. Because the nature of these organizations, their size and range of activities, and their financial reporting practices all vary, they constitute a useful selection to acquaint our team with current practice in financial reporting by nonprofit entities.

An Overview of the Illustrative Statements
Each of the three sets of financial statements has been subjected to audit "in accordance with generally accepted

auditing standards." The audits of the American Accounting Association and the American Association of Retired Persons were performed by firms of independent certified public accountants. The audit of the State of Utah was performed by the Office of the State Auditor. The State Auditor is an elected official, a CPA, and his letterhead shows the Director of Audit and five Audit Managers, all as CPAs.

In each case, the auditors' opinion contains the words "present fairly, in all material respects," and "in conformity with generally accepted accounting principles."

The form of presentation of the financial statements varies substantially among the three organizations. The American Accounting Association and the State of Utah use columnar arrangements to present the details for different funds. The American Association of Retired Persons' financial statements refer to fund balances but they neither report fund details nor identify any funds. Thus AARP has no need for a columnar format. Its financial statements are similar in form to those of a business corporation.

The extent of disclosure in each set of statements is impressive. In addition to the basic financial statements--a balance sheet, operating statement, and a statement of cash flows--extensive footnotes are appended including a number of schedules as well as comments and explanations.

In contrast to the extent of disclosure, there appears little effort to make the financial statements understandable to unsophisticated readers. Technical terms are used liberally. Explanations of such terms are nonexistent.

Considerable emphasis on funds is found in the statements of the American Accounting Association and the State of Utah. Their reports are built around fund distinctions clearly set out in the columnar structure of the statements. The American Association of Retired Persons' statements refer to "fund balances" but, other than distingishing "designated" and "undesignated" funds, provide no details on a fund basis.

Each of the three not-for-profit entities engages in some activities that at least appear to be conducted on a for-profit basis. Only the State of Utah reports income statements for such activities independent of its other activities.

The American Accounting Association

The American Accounting Association is the professional organization of academic accountants. Over the years it has been a significant force for improvement in accounting theory and practice. Its membership is open and includes practicing CPAs and accountants in industry and government as well as academics.

The American Accounting Association's Financial Statements

The American Accounting Association has the least complex activities of the three organizations. Its financial statements include:

1. Comparative BALANCE SHEETS for two years.
2. Comparative STATEMENTS OF SUPPORT AND REVENUE, EXPENSES AND CHANGES IN FUND BALANCES for two years.
3. Comparative STATEMENTS OF CASH FLOWS for two years.
4. NOTES TO FINANCIAL STATEMENTS.

Each of these financial statements is prepared on a columnar basis showing:
August 31, 1991
    General Fund

Designated
    Sections Funds
    Regions Funds
Restricted
    Fellowship Funds
Total All Funds
August 31, 1990
    General Funds
    Total All Funds

The Balance Sheet includes details and totals for each of the four funds and Total All Funds for Current Assets, Other Assets, Total Assets, Current Liabilities, Other Liabilities, Fund Balance, and Total Liabilities and Fund Balance.

The Statement of Support and Revenue, Expenses and Changes in Fund Balances includes details and totals for Support and Revenue, Expenses, Excess (Deficiency) of Support and Revenue Over (Under) Expenses, and Fund Balances Beginning and End of Year.

The Statement of Cash Flows includes details and totals for Cash Flows from Operating Activities, Cash Flows from Investing Activities, Cash Flows from Financing Activities, Net Increase (Decrease) in Cash and Cash Equivalents, and Cash and Cash Equivalents Beginning and End of Year.

The Notes to Financial Statements have the following sections:

Note 1-Summary of Significant Accounting Policies.
Note 2-Description of Funds.
Note 3-Cash and Cash Equivalents.
Note 4-Property and Equipment.
Note 5-Employee Benefit Plan.
Note 6-Employment Agreement.
Note 7-Major Program-Revenues and Expenses.

Some Consulting Team Comments

Having reviewed the American Accounting Association report, one team member suggested that mixing profit-directed and not-for-profit activities together didn't make much sense. "If there is a chance that different financial accounting principles apply to these different kinds of activities, shouldn't we keep them separate? And for the profit-directed activities, I think we ought to match up related costs and revenues. Note that when you match up the expenses for 'Annual Convention' with the revenue for the same item, you have a $100,000 profit. Looks like those who attend the annual convention are subsidizing some of the Association's other activities. Seems to me, good reporting should show this."

Another team member noted the separation of "unrestricted" from "designated or restricted" funds, but with no indication of the nature or extent of the restrictions. "What's the use of telling readers that funds are "restricted" or "designated" if you don't tell them what those terms mean? How are they "restricted" and for what are they "designated?" Another team member disagreed. He felt that even a reader with little or no familiarity with such terms could tell that the funds designated for sections, regions, and fellowships were intended for specific purposes, and the general fund took care of those funds whose use was not limited. In his view, the Association was sufficiently uncomplicated that anyone interested could understand the meaning of those terms. "And besides," he held, "'Note 2--Description of Funds' explains those terms well enough for anyone."

Another comment was directed at the Statement of Cash Flows. "I've always had trouble with this statement and its three sections. Why must the Association stick with a format that doesn't seem to meet its needs?"

"If you want to be pickie," said another member, "you could decide that the property and equipment included with the assets are cash-consuming rather than cash-producing resources. As such, they should not be included in a total with those properties that are or will produce cash. But to tell the truth, in an organization like this I'm not sure it makes any real difference."

"Oh, it's just another example of sloppy reporting" came a response from another voice. "I'm a member of the AAA. Have been for years. But I never really looked at its financial statements before. I guess I had no reason to do so. But look at that item for 'Research and education. . . $750.' This is an academic organization. Most of what it does relates directly or indirectly to either education or research. Judging from its classification of expenses, one might think one of its major activities is 'Administration.' Note that amount of $666,069 for 'Administration' compared with the measly amount for 'Research and Education.' And this from an organization of *accountants*. If I were at home, I'd write someone a letter!"

The American Association of Retired Persons

The team leader introduced the financial statements of the American Association of Retired Persons with these words: "This is a remarkable, and remarkably complex, not-for-profit(?) organization. An outsider is at a loss to describe it adequately. The AARP makes its extensive membership list available to selected independent companies which have a product or service that the AARP believes its members might desire. By negotiating favorable terms on which the independent company is permitted to offer such services to AARP members, the AARP provides its members a unique service. By including in such negotiations a payment for advertising, royalties, sales efforts, and/or similar activities, the AARP increases its total revenues substantially, and is thereby able to provide its members with additional benefits.

"In addition, the AARP apparently owns and operates a number of other profit-directed companies.

"The AARP is thus an example of a nominally nonprofit organization that engages in significant profit-directed activities. The profits so derived are used for purposes directly or indirectly beneficial to its members. If the AARP has stockholders, that is not apparent from its balance sheet. If anyone "owns" the organization, it has to be the members. Yet they have no equity in the sense of an interest they can sell. To benefit from any "profits," they must continue as members and accept whatever benefits the management decides the members should receive."

The American Association of Retired Persons' Financial Statements

The AARP's financial statements include:

1. Comparative CONSOLIDATED BALANCE SHEETS for two years.
2. Comparative CONSOLIDATED STATEMENTS OF REVENUES, EXPENSES, AND CHANGES IN FUND BALANCES for two years.
3. Comparative CONSOLIDATED STATEMENTS OF CASH FLOWS for two years.

These financial statements resemble closely those of business corporations. The major difference in the Consolidated Balance Sheets is that their equity sections are entitled "Fund Balances" and include an amount described as "Designated by Board of Directors" and another described as "Undesignated." The Consolidated Statements of Revenues, Expenses and Changes in Fund Balances arrive at a "bottom line" of "(Deficiency) excess of revenues over expenses." This amount is then affected by "Amount (deducted from) added to undesignated funds." The result is added to the "Undesignated Fund Balance," beginning of year to arrive at the "Undesignated Fund Balance," end of year.

The Consolidated Statements of Cash Flows follow the standard format.

If the AARP has distinct funds, these are not apparent in its financial statements. The term "funds" is used but no fund distinctions are disclosed. Except for a distinction between "Designated by Board of Directors" and "Undesignated" as described above, there is very little information about funds.

The NOTES TO FINANCIAL STATEMENTS include these sections:

Description of Organization
Significant Accounting Policies
AARP Financial Services Corp. and AARP Service
    Company
Furniture and Equipment
Government Grants
AARP Insurance Plan
Operating Expenses
Income from Other Programs and Services
Health Care Benefits
Commitments and Contingencies
Pension Plan

Team Members' Reactions

How did our team of consultants react after perusing the AARP financial statements? They concluded the report was remarkably similar to those of business corporations. Further, given the nature of the AARP's activities, they saw no reason why its annual report should differ from that of a business corporation. They also found that the combination of forprofit and nonprofit activities is such that determining the success of the forprofit activities alone is somewhere between difficult and impossible with the amount of information provided. If related revenues and expenses are associated to show their relationship to one another, the report does not make this clear. And the AARP's financial statements do not separate its business activities from its nonprofit activities in such a way that a reader can discover which dominates the other.

As with the financial statements of the American Accounting Association, no distinction is made between cash-consuming and cash-producing properties. The lengthy footnotes provide considerable information but would certainly daunt any but a financially trained and very determined reader. One wonders what proportion of the AARP's membership could possibly understand them. One member of the team suggested these financial statements were probably prepared because they were necessary for the conduct of the AARP's business activities, not to inform its members.

The State of Utah's Financial Statements

The State of Utah's *Comprehensive Annual Report* is probably representative of the ultimate in fund accounting and reporting. In total, 54 funds and two account groups are reported in some detail. Technically, the General Purpose Financial Statements for the State of Utah referred to in this chapter include only seven fund types, two account groups, and one added column for a component unit, Colleges and Universities. However, details are presented in one schedule or another for 54 funds and two account groups as described. The report also includes a "Certificate of Excellence in Financial Reporting" presented by the Government Finance Officers Association of the United States and Canada "...to government and public employee retirement systems whose comprehensive annual reports (CAFRS's) achieve the highest standards in government accounting and financial reporting."

An overwhelming amount of detailed information is thus presented, more than enough to discourage most general purpose readers. No attempt to emphasize some small number of important financial facts is found in the formal report. However, included within the same covers are four pages of "Financial Highlights" utilizing charts and graphs for comparison purposes. Tracing the figures used in the highlights section into the formal statements calls for both skill and understanding that few readers will possess.

Included within the Comprehensive Financial Report are the following formal financial statements, each in a columnar format with column headings as shown:

1. Combined Balance Sheet, All Fund Types and
   Account Groups
   > Government Fund Types
   >> General
   >> Special Revenue
   >> Capital Projects
   >> Debt Service
   > Proprietary Fund Types
   >> Enterprise
   >> Internal Service
   > Fiduciary Fund Types
   >> Trust and Agency
   > Account Groups
   >> General Fixed Assets
   >> General Long-Term Obligations
   > College and University Funds
   > Total (Memorandum Only) June 30, 1991
   > Total (Memorandum Only) June 30, 1990

2. Combined Statement of Revenues, Expenditures,
   and Changes in Fund Balances:
   > Government Fund Types
   >> General

Special Revenue
Capital Projects
Debt Service
Fiduciary Fund Types
Expendable Trust
Total (Memorandum Only) June 30, 1991
Total (Memorandum Only) June 30, 1990

3. Combined Statement of Revenues, Expenditures, and Changes in Fund Balances--Budget and Actual (Budgetary Basis); General Fund, Special Revenue Funds, and Debt Service Fund:
General Fund
Budget
Actual
Variance, Favorable (Unfavorable)
Special Revenue Funds
Budget
Actual
Variance, Favorable (Unfavorable)
Debt Service Fund
Budget
Actual
Variance, Favorable (Unfavorable)

4. Combined Statement of Revenues, Expenses, and Changes in Retained Earnings/Fund Balances--All Proprietary Fund Types and Similar Trust Funds
Proprietary Fund Types
Enterprise
Internal Service
Fiduciary Fund Types
Non-expendable
Pension Trust

5. Combined Statement of Cash Flows--All Proprietary Fund Types and Nonexpendable Trust Fund:
      Proprietary Fund Types
          Enterprise
          Internal Service
      Fiduciary Fund Types
          Non-expendable Trust

6. Combined Statement of Current Funds Revenues, Expenditures, and Other Changes--Colleges and Universities:
      Total Unrestricted
      Total Restricted
      Total Current Funds

7. Combined Statement of Changes in Fund Balances --College and University Fund Types:
      Current Funds
          Unrestricted
          Restricted
      Loan Funds
      Endowment Funds
      Plant Funds
          Unexpended
          Renewal and Replacement
          Retirement of Indebtedness
          Investment in Plant
      Foundation and Institutes

8. FOOTNOTES TO FINANCIAL STATEMENTS (constituting 32 pages of small print and including both text and many schedules)
      Note 1. Summary of significant accounting policies
          A. Reporting Entity
          B. Fund Accounting
          C. Basis of Accounting

D. Budgeting and Budgetary Control
E. Cash and Cash Equivalents and Investments
F. Receivables
G. Advances to Other Funds
H. Inter/Intrafund Transactions
I. Inventories
J. Fixed Assets
K. Deferred Charges
L. Accrued Liabilities
M   Deferred Revenues
N. Contractor Retention
O. Policy Claim Liabilities
P. Grants
Q. Bond Discounts/Issuance Costs
R. Fund Equity
S. Retirement and Employee Benefit Costs
T. Compensated Absences
U. Long-Term Obligations
V. Totals (memorandum only)

Note 2. Beginning Fund Balance Adjustment and Other Changes

Note 3. Deposits and Investments
A. Deposits
B. Reverse Repurchase Agreements
C. Investments

Note 4. Due From/To Other Funds

Note 5. General Fixed Assets

Note 6. Lease Commitments

Note 7. Bonds and Notes Payable
A. General Obligation Bonds

    B. Revenue Bonds
    C. Notes Payable
    D. Contracts Payable
    E. Leave Obligations

Note 8. Fund Balances--Reserved and Designated
    A. General Fund--Reserved
    B. Special Revenue Funds--Reserved
    C. Capital Projects Fund
    D. Trust and Agency Funds
    E. Internal Service Funds
    F. Enterprise Funds

Note 9. Deficit Fund Balances/Retained Earnings

Note 10. Changes in Contributed Capital Accounts

Note 11. Operating and Residual Equity Transfers

Note 12. Segment Information for Enterprise Funds

Note 13. Litigation Contingencies, and Commitments

Note 14. Pension Plans
    A. Utah State Retirement Systems
    B. Teachers Insurance and Annuity Association
    C. Travelers Insurance Retirement Plan

Note 15. Deferred Compensation Plan

Note 16. Post Employment Benefits

Note 17. Risk Management and Insurance

Note 18. Subsequent Events

To get some idea of the extent of detail provided in these various financial statements, please note that the Combined Balance Sheet, All Fund Types and Account Groups, includes line item amounts for each of the following:

Assets
    Cash and Cash Equivalents (Notes 2,3)
    Investments (Notes 1, 2, 3)
    Receivables:
        Accounts (Note 1)
        Notes/Mortgages (Note 1)
        Accrued Interest
        Unbilled
    Due From Other Funds
    Advance to Other Funds
    Inventories
    Prepaid Items
    Deferred Charges
    Deferred Compensation Plan Assets (Note 15)
    Land (Note 1)
    Buildings and Improvements (Note 1)
    Machinery and Equipment (Note 1)
        Accumulated Depreciation
    Construction-In-Progress
    Amount in Debt Service Fund
    Resources to be Provided in Future Years For:
        Retirement of General Obligation Bonds
        Other General Long-Term Obligations
    Total Assets
Liability, Equity, and Other Credits

Vouchers Payable
Contracts Payable
Accrued Liabilities
Obligations Under Reverse Repurchase Agree
ments
Deposits
Due to Other Funds (Note 4)
Due to Other Individuals or Groups
Due to Other Taxing Units
Deferred Revenue
Advance From Other Funds
Policy Claim Liabilities
Notes Payable (Note 7)
General Obligation Bonds Payable (Note 7)
Revenue Bonds Payable (Note 7)
Leave Obligations (Notes 1, 7)
Deferred Compensation Plan Liability (Note 15)
    Total Liabilities

Equity and Other Credits:
Contributed Working Capital
Investment in Fixed Assets
Retained Earnings
Fund Balances:
    Reserved (Note 8)
    Unreserved Designated
    Unreserved Undesignated
        Total Equity and Other Credits
Total Liabilities, Equity, and Other Credits

The Combined Statement of Revenues, Expenditures, and Changes in Fund Balances, All Governmental Fund Types and Expendable Trust Funds, includes the following items:

Revenues:
Unrestricted:

        Sales Tax
        Individual Income Tax
        Corporate Tax
        Motor and Special Fuel Tax
        Licenses, Permits, and Fees
        Interest on Investments
        Miscellaneous Taxes and Other
            Total Unrestricted
    Restricted:
        Federal Grants and Contracts
        Departmental Collections
        Aeronautics
        Federal Mineral Lease
        Intergovernmental Revenues
        Interest on Investments
        Premiums/Other Collections
        Miscellaneous
            Total Restricted
            Total Revenues

Expenditures:
    Current:
        General Government
        Human Services
        Corrections
        Health
        Higher Education
        Natural Resources
        Business, Labor, and Agriculture
        Community and Economic Development
        Unemployment Claims
        Public Education
        Transportation and Public Safety
    Capital Outlay
    Debt Service:
        Principal Retirement
        Interest and Other Charges

Total Expenditures
Excess Revenues Over (Under) Expenditures

Other Financing Sources (Uses):
    Proceeds of Revenue Bonds/Contracts
    Proceeds of General Obligation Bonds
    Operating Transfers In (Note 11)
    Operating Transfers Out (Note 11)
        Total Other Financing Sources (Uses)

Excess Revenues and Other Sources Over (Under)
 Expenditures and Other Uses

Beginning Fund Balances
Residual Equity Transfers (Note 11)
Ending Fund Balances

Comments by Members of the Consulting Team

Two features of the *Comprehensive Annual Report* impressed the team members the most. First was the extent of disclosure. To those who had never reviewed such a report before, the total amount of information presented was both a surprise and overwhelming. This led to the second impression, the difficulty of comprehending the meaning of all the information presented. One wag commented: "I'd give them an 'A' on disclosure and an 'F' on understandability. With all this mass of detail, can anyone tell me just how well the State of Utah is doing?" Another member commented: "I feel like I've been trying to drink from a fire hose. Perhaps that's the point in all this disclosure. It's both beyond criticism and beyond understanding."

The free use of unexplained technical terms and the need to study carefully the lengthy footnotes discouraged interest. Team members also raised questions about the purpose in preparing the *Comprehensive Annual Report*.

For whom was it prepared? Not very many citizens are technically competent to find their way through such a document, even if they had the time and the desire to do so. As a source of information for the executive and legislative officers of the State and their staffs, the report should have usefulness. But publication implies intent for some form of general distribution. In fact the Report is addressed to "The Citizens, Governor, and Members of the Legislature of the State of Utah." A reader interested only in how well the State is doing in meeting its budget and keeping out of debt might have a very hard time in finding answers to his or her questions.

It was something of a surprise to some team members to discover that the State was engaged in profit-directed activities, or at least in recovering costs. Such efforts are fully disclosed and there appears to be an appropriate association of related revenues and expenses. Insofar as a reader can determine from the terms and fund titles used, sufficient information is available to separate the State's "business activities" from its governmental activities.

Team Member Impressions Over All

When asked to state what impressed them most in the financial reports of the three entities as a group, varying opinions were expressed by the team members. Their views ran generally to the following:

1. The apparent variety of activities and financial reporting within the nonprofit class.

2. The extent to which nonprofit entities engaged in forprofit activities.

3. The complexity of fund accounting when carried to the degree found in the State of Utah report.

4. The freedom apparently permitted when "generally accepted accounting principles" are applied to nonprofit entities.

5. The absence of a "bottom line" item of any kind to indicate "success" or failure.

6. The absence of any identifiable purpose of the reporting.

7. Confusion as to the anticipated readership of these reports.

8. The apparent lack of interest in the differences between forprofit and nonprofit entities, differences that had been considered of fundamental importance to the team members in their discussion of nonprofit financial reporting.

CHAPTER 3
SOME PROBLEMS
OF ACCOUNTING THEORY

We left our consulting team at the end of Chapter 1 in the early stages of its assignment while it, and we, took some time to familiarize ourselves with examples of current practice in financial reporting by nonprofit entities. After doing so, the team resumed its deliberations working toward final recommendations to be made to its client. As you might expect, there was a difference of opinion within the committee on the nature of those recommendations. Some members argued for rather detailed rules and prescribed formats; others held out for general statements of principle. A complete replay of their arguments and discussions would be both entertaining and informative. It would also be lengthy and at times tedious. In the interests of time, a summary of their exchanges on the more important matters may serve our purpose satisfactorily.

A rather small number of issues received major attention. Most of these were identified early in the study; some others appeared later. A summary of the nature of each of these, their importance in the development of final recommendations, and the reasons why the team took the position it did on each of these is all we have time for here. These key issues are:

1. The nature and importance of differences between business organizations and nonprofit entities.

2. The applicability of conventional accounting concepts to nonprofit entities.

3. The applicability of conventional financial statement formats to nonprofit entities.

4. The feasibility of the fund emphasis for financial reporting purposes.

5. The nature and importance of differences among nonprofit entities.

Differences Between Business and Nonprofit Organizations

Two members of the team had been given the assignment of developing the differences between business corporations and nonprofit organizations and the influence of those differences on accounting and financial reporting. They presented the summary shown on page 43 to the group.

Importance of Differences

The authors of the table supplemented their summary with the following explanation.

"In business and not-for-profit entities, we have organizations that differ in purpose, operations, viability, use of resources, interrelationships among the interests involved, and in the kinds of decision information useful to those interests.

"Conceptually, the differences between business and not-for-profit organizations are so important they cannot be ignored. Generally accepted accounting principles have been carefully developed over many years to serve an interest, equity ownership, that has dominated business

Differences Between Business and Nonprofit Organizations

ATTRIB-UTE	BUSINESS	NONPROFIT
Purpose	Profit for owners.	Service to beneficiaries at no cost or below cost.
Operations	Production and sale of products and/or services at a price to exceed cost to make and sell.	(1) Fund raising; (2) providing services.
Measures of success	Amount of profit; return on investment; financial condition.	Percent of receipts expended for stated purpose. Amount of funds obtained.
Viability	Depends on customer satisfaction with quality, price, and service.	Depends on success of fund raising and control of expenditures.
Purpose of resources	Intended and expected to be used in operations to generate cash in excess of cost, thereby providing for their replacement.	Intended and expected to be used to provide services distributed gratis or below cost.
Interests and relationships	Equity interest expects profits and protection of equity; management is subject to investor control; customer satisfaction is essential; creditors and employees have interests of varying strength.	Contributors/tax-payers are essential; management subject to control only under extreme conditions in solicitation organizations, and to political control in government organizations.
Decision information	Amount of profit, return on equity, ratio of debt to equity.	Proportion of receipts utilized, nature of expenditures, extent of present and future need for receipts.

organizations but does not exist in not-for-profit entities. In addition, those principles focus on income measurement, a focus irrelevant to entities lacking a profit motive.

"The basic definition in business accounting theory is that for assets. Assets are acquired with the expectation that they will provide a positive cash flow over their lifetimes. But many of the properties of a nonprofit organization are used for purposes different from the purposes of a business; such properties are expected to cause a net cash outflow over their lives. Finally, the nature of the decisions to be made by investors in a business entity are entirely different from the kinds of decisions to be made by the interests in a nonprofit organization."

Following up on the comments of those who had prepared the table and explained its importance, the team leader suggested: "With all of these differences, perhaps we should give some attention to the applicability of conventional generally accepted accounting principles to not-for-profit organizations. Let's begin by examining the "building blocks" of accounting theory, the basic concepts."

Nonprofit Organizations and the Basic Accounting Concepts

The FASB describes five concepts as the basic building blocks of accounting theory: assets, liabilities, equity, revenue, and expense. The team considered each of these from the point of view of a not-for-profit organization.

Assets (and Service Facilities). Certainly a nonprofit organization must have assets. For example, we saw in the illustrations in Chapter 2 that such entities have cash, investments, receivables, and inventory. But a nonprofit entity may also have properties that look like assets, are essential to the entity's operations, and were costly to acquire--but they were not acquired with either the intention or the anticipation that they will provide a net cash inflow over time. Remember the illustration cited by a team member in Chapter 1, the municipal bus company that never made a profit.[1]Consider also such properties as municipal buildings, state parks, the Federal highway system, cathedrals, and public monuments. None of these is expected to yield a net cash inflow over its life, yet each is valuable, acquired knowingly, important to the owning organization's purpose--and a cash consumer.

Think what happens when we include such properties with other properties that do meet the requirements of an asset. For example, add the cost, or current market value, of investments in marketable securities to the cost of properties held to provide free temporary housing to homeless transients. What useful information does the resulting total yield? How can it be described in any understandable fashion? Adding cash-producing property to cash-consuming property is almost like adding assets and liabilities. One brings cash in, the other sends cash out. One property meets the definition of an asset, the other does not.

Nonprofits typically require and own cash-consuming properties. If a business organization owned a property that had the expectation of a continuing net outflow of cash indefinitely into the future, the business would view the property not as an asset but as a loss to be disposed of as quickly as possible. But such a property is not a loss to a nonprofit entity. It helps the nonprofit realize the purpose of its existence.[2]

This raises the question: What is a cash-consuming property if it is neither an asset nor a loss? First, a property intentionally acquired to be cash consuming represents a concept completely foreign to generally accepted accounting principles. It has the effect of a liability, but who ever heard of a liability with a debit balance? Of course a cash-consuming property fails to meet the definition of a liability just as it fails to meet the definition of an asset. In terms of effect, however, it is closer to a liability than to an asset. For lack of a better term, think of it as a "service facility," something that has all the qualities of an asset except the intent and ability (in its present use) to produce a net cash inflow over time.

Liabilities (and Commitments). Just as a nonprofit entity has assets, it can also have liabilities, both short and long-term. It also has commitments. And, as explained at length elsewhere,[3] these have an important influence on the nonprofit entity's viability. For example, when a nonprofit organization acquires a major service facility, it does so because the facility is essential to its purpose. If the facility is long-lived, continuation of the service will require maintaining and staffing the facility throughout its useful life, and ultimately either renovating or replacing it. Thus the acquisition of a service facility or the institution of a program of services commits the nonprofit organization to continue the service or the program until future developments provide cause to change policy. Of course such entities may have other commitments as well. Some of these may be firm plans that have not yet reached the contract stage; others may be contingent on favorable developments and can readily be cancelled.

   Liabilities are commitments, but not all commitments are liabilities. A change in policy can rearrange a nonprofit entity's commitments in short order. Doesn't it then seem reasonable that those persons making contributions or paying taxes to such an entity, if they are to have sufficient information to determine whether to continue contributing or to take political action, need to know something about the entity's commitments? The team members were all in the affirmative on that question.

What they could not agree on was how to report commitments, or even if financial statements provided a way to do so.

Equity. The term "equity" implies ultimate ownership in a business organization. Included within that ownership are a number of rights and privileges including the right to claim net income, to have the organization managed for the financial benefit of its owners, to dispose of that ownership interest, to have a voice in choosing management, and so on. No similar interest exists in a nonprofit. Some members of the consulting team tried to draw an analogy between the interests of contributors and/or taxpayers and the equity interest of shareholders in a corporation. But they found the attacks of other members who pointed out the fundamental inaccuracies in the analogy too hard to meet. Ultimately, general agreement prevailed within the team: the conventional concept of equity has no place in financial reporting for nonprofit organizations.

And that led to another question. If the difference between the total assets and the total liabilities is not equity, just what is it? One of the team members noted that in the nonprofit entity financial statements they had seen, the term "fund balance" was used to describe that amount and to provide balance sheets with equal debits and credits. This led to a brief discussion of the meaning of "fund balance." What information could the words "fund balance" possibly convey to users of the financial statements? "Why don't we just call the difference between assets and liabilities 'net assets?' After all, that's what it is." This from one of the less voluble members of the team put the issue to rest.

Of course one of the humorists in the group noted "It's a good thing we aren't doing this for the good old USA. 'Net liabilities' has a connotation of bankruptcy."

Revenue. Are contributions received and taxes collected properly described as "revenue"? Some members of the team felt they were not. To them, use of the term "revenue" implied earning, that is, performing some service or providing a product to a customer or client in return for which the customer or client made payment. In their view, the activities of a nonprofit and its relationship with contributors and beneficiaries was not such as to constitute the kind of earning that "revenue" implied. They suggested an emphasis on "receipts" was more appropriate, and they recommended terms like "contributions received" and "taxes received." Other members could see the point but did not think anyone reading the financial statements of a nonprofit would be misled by use of the term "revenue." The consensus was that "receipts" was the more appropriate designation but that "revenue" was not sufficently misleading to rule out its use by those who preferred it.

Expense. A similar distinction was suggested for "expense" and "expenditure," the former implying an effort made to obtain income, the latter signifying only an outlay of cash. The conclusion was much the same as in the revenue/receipt argument. "Expenditure" was regarded as more accurate, but there was a strong suspicion that requiring its use would be a refinement few would recognize or follow.

SOME ADDITIONAL CONCEPTUAL QUESTIONS

Matching.

A considerable amount of time was spent by the team discussing "matching," a term much used in accounting but not always well understood. One of the older team members who prided himself on being something of a theorist insisted that the term had been introduced by Paton and Littleton in the 1930's. In his graduate theory courses, Littleton sometimes described expenses as "efforts to obtain revenue" and revenue, then, as the "accomplishments" that resulted from those efforts. To determine whether "efforts" had been successful, they must be matched with the related "accomplishments." This could be done on the basis of specific efforts and accomplishments such as the costs and revenues for a given construction project, for a retail store, or for a department or other segment, or more generally in an entity's income statement for a year.

Although he could not quote a specific reference, the team member's own belief was that matching was best understood as the "useful association of related data in financial statements." Thus he argued that if a service entity also engaged in some profit-directed activities, the cost of each of these activities should be matched with the revenues or receipts resulting therefrom. This would be done in an income statement if the activity were of sufficient materiality, or, for less material items, in a two-line presentation (revenues minus expenses) in the organization's operating statement. He would also accept a netting of related expenses against revenue, or vice versa, for items of minimum materiality.

The other members of the team found this a useful idea. His success encouraged the proponent of this view to launch on a theoretical discussion of the pros and cons of allocating joint expenses among several revenues based on his experience as a staff member for the Cost Accounting Standards Board, but at this point his colleagues lost all interest.

Similarities versus Differences

In a late evening conversation, a team member who had spent some time on the staff of the FASB during the

completion of its "Conceptual Framework Project" expressed concern that the team seemed to be moving
toward suggesting different accounting standards for
nonprofit organizations than for business organizations.
Indeed, he was disturbed by the very fact that developing
accounting standards for nonprofit entities had been
assigned to a different team than had the standards for
business organizations.

He recognized that differences existed between business and not-for-profit entities, but what was more
important was that both kinds of organization go to a
single pool of capital for loans and equity capital. Thus
they were in competition for the same resources. Unless
they all reported in compliance with the same accounting
standards, one or the other might receive an unintended
and socially undesirable advantage.

This was a point of view not previously considered by
the team, one that seemed to question everything it had
resolved to date. At least it did until one of the quiet
members of the team broke the silence with a series of
questions:

"Just how big is this single pool of capital? Do you
mean that when I financed most of the price of my last
new car, I was competing with some Fortune 500
company that was trying to float a new issue of bonds?
Or now that we emphasize the international aspects of
business, was I also competing for credit with companies
in Japan and Germany? In theory, I suppose there is
something in what you say. Practically, it doesn't make
a lot of sense.

"Let's not forget that nonprofit entities have no equity
interest. People don't contribute to charities or governments like they invest in business. The pool of capital for
which business corporations compete is all investment
capital. People make contributions and pay taxes for
entirely different reasons than they make investments.
The motivations are so different from those that influence

investments that it is hard to conceive of a single pool of capital including both.

"Of course both businesses and not-for-profit organizations borrow from time to time, and that may be on a competitive basis. But picture yourself as the banker evaluating those competing applications. What would you look for? The business would provide a series of income statements and balance sheets. You would be interested in its continuing profitability and the possible sale value of its assets. The nonprofit entity would give you a record of its fund-raising success over several past years, and perhaps a list of its assets and service facilities. That record of its receipts would not be an income statement nor subject to the same accounting standards. You would be interested in the present debts of both organizations, and in their ability to meet them, of course, and accounting principles are important in assuring that debt is fairly stated. We need to keep that idea in mind. I expect service facilities would be of relatively little interest although the nonprofit's resources could be important. But I don't see the banker spending much time comparing the balance sheet of a business corporation with the balance sheet of a nonprofit entity. His real interest in the not-for-profit would be its flow of receipts.

"So I don't see that single pool of capital idea nearly as important as I see the differences between the two kinds of entities. What I do see as possible, even probable, are some different ways of presenting a not-for-profit's operations and financial condition."

Not everyone was immediately convinced by this mini-lecture, but they all became a little more curious about their final report. Some members even began to experiment with pro forma statements quite different from anything they had ever visualized before.

Financial Statement Formats

The late night conversation just referred to tended to focus the team's interest on appropriate financial statement formats somewhat sooner than otherwise might have occurred. An important difference of opinion occurred when a member suggested that most not-for-profit organizations were involved in two different and not closely related activities.

Two Major Activities. This proposal can be traced directly back to discussions of matching and to the importance of differences. In a conversation involving only two members, one of them suggested that the differences between fund-raising and service provision by a nonprofit were probably such that matching the costs of the latter with the receipts of the former would be inappropriate. His companion agreed and added that the costs of fund-raising certainly should be matched with the results, that is with the receipts obtained. This led to questioning what the cost of services provided might be matched against. The easy answer, they agreed, is to match the cost of providing services with the accomplishments that follow. Unfortunately, given the purpose of nonprofits and the nature of their activities, few of them would have an objective market figure for services delivered.

Further conversation suggested that possibly there were no measurable results with the present state of the art, but perhaps with more experience, ways of measuring such results might be developed. And that possibility was then proposed as another reason for encouraging separate development of nonprofit financial reporting.

"If we accountants are content to treat all costs incurred by the nonprofit entity as expenses and all receipts as revenues, and if we then combine these in a single-step operating statement a la business accounting, we will never even consider exploring the measurement of accomplishments for such entities."

"But are we agreed that the not-for-profit really is involved in two different activities? First, it raises funds either by seeking contributions or through taxation; then, in a not completely unrelated activity, it spends the funds raised to provide services. So the two activities are related" contended his associate. "Both are involved with the same funds. The funds are the tie between them."

"Well, not in the sense that either one causes the other. Fund-raising permits services, it doesn't cause the services. Providing services expends the funds, it doesn't bring them in. There is a relationship, but it is nothing like the effort/accomplishment relationship we talked about as relating expenses to income in a business organization."

"Now hold on just a minute. Of course some expenses cause receipts for nonprofits. Think of the fund-raising efforts in an alumni association. And if the nonprofit recognizes pledges as assets, it will have some uncollectibles. These certainly constitute an expense caused by fundraising. So there are some matchings of receipts and expenses that should be shown in an operating statement. Now I think I can agree with you that a nonprofit is indeed engaged in two separate activities. But the main reason for reporting on either one of these activities is to show the effect on net assets. Receipts bring in net assets; providing services to beneficiaries consumes net assets. Readers of financial statements want to know both facts: how much was received and how much was spent. And the difference between these is another useful fact. That difference is important as a measure of the change in net assets for the year.

"As a reader of the entity's financial statements, I would want to know the change in net assets for the year. Wouldn't you? If it is a very large positive figure, it raises questions about whether the entity is actually using the contributions received for the stated purpose. If it isn't doing so, why should I make another contribution? If the difference is a large negative figure, then I wonder if the entity can long survive. Does the management know what it is doing if it can't hold its expenditures in line with its receipts? The more I think about it, the more I think we need an operating statement that shows the entity's change in net assets for the year."

When these two brought their views on financial reporting to the rest of the team the next day, most of the other members opted for an operating statement that reported the change in net assets for the year. Most of them also agreed that with the right use of descriptions there was little danger than anyone would consider such an amount as a measure of success like net income.

They also found some of the members of the team anxious to consider another concern: "The real problem in developing an operating statement for a nonprofit is that you have to have so many of them. With all these funds to be reported, we need an operating statement for each one of them. Do you remember the number of funds the State of Utah has? Its Annual Financial Report is overwhelming. We need to give some attention to the sheer mass of reported information. There aren't many people I know who have the patience to work their way through all those fund statements.

Fund Financial Reporting

At this point a puzzled voice broke in: "Will someone please explain to me what the advantage of all these funds columns in the financial statements is? I know that some gifts and certain taxes are restricted to specified uses, and I know that fund accounting is useful to help management avoid overspending or using restricted money for improper purposes. But when I was reading the State's annual report, the thought came to me that no reader could assimilate all that information. What that report gives us is a financial jig saw puzzle with no picture on the pieces to help the reader put the puzzle together. Only a career specialist with some inside information can really make much out of all that fractionated information.

"Further, it occurred to me that if anyone wanted to discourage readers, fractionating the State's financial information into all those columns would be a wonderful way to do it. I don't accuse anyone of such a trick, but I can't help being suspicious. Why can't the state auditor just make a general statement that all expenditures have been restricted to funds appropriate for the purpose expended? That's all the average reader wants to know about funds anyway. Now am I crazy, or does someone agree with me?"

This outburst destroyed any organized discussion for a few minutes. It also set the team's thinking in a new direction. The first reaction was one of mild derision. That reaction slowly changed as each team member remembered the frustration he had felt in trying to absorb the quantity of detailed information in the State's report. Some had commented on the much less complicated but still fund-oriented report of the American Accounting Association. Accountants reading financial statements could probably manage a few funds without difficulty, but not all nonprofit statements were prepared for accountants. And some nonprofits reported more than "a few" funds. Just how many readers of financial statements were sufficiently interested in that extent of detail to justify its presentation? More important, to what extent did the quantity of detail get in the way of an understanding of the overall picture? Who could read those reports and then say readily and with authority whether an association or a state had improved its financial situation over the year? Or whether it had achieved its financial purposes?

During that discussion, one of the team members who had worked on some government audits ventured the thought that one of the reasons for emphasizing fund distinctions was the non-fungibility of fund resources. The assets in Fund A might not be available to satisfy the debts of Fund B. If readers saw only one amount for "Cash," they would likely assume that all of it was available for whatever purpose management wished to use it. Actually, such an assumption would be contrary to the facts of life for many nonprofits.

Slowly but surely a consensus emerged. If the report were for members of an association or the citizens of a state, simplicity was essential. Those users involved in management might need substantial detail, especially those concerned with a specific fund. But the people not concerned with specific funds, those to whom the reports were at least nominally addressed, were far more likely to be distracted and discouraged by the surfeit of detail than to be helped. An explanatory footnote could easily make the point about non-fungibility and the limitations of general purpose financial statements. Further, without the necessity of reporting on each individual fund in the general purpose statements, the freedom to experiment with unconventional but more relevant financial presentations was enhanced considerably.

Another Difference Between Business and Not-for-Profit Entities

In the heated process of reaching that consensus, a remark by one of the less vocal members was almost lost. He had said something like "One thing about leaving out some of this detail, the accountants are not likely to be sued." But the team leader had heard that comment and made a note to discuss it later.   When he did find the right opportunity, he suggested to the full committee that this casual comment might actually have some bearing on the nature of the team's conclusions.

"This country is accustomed to tight control exercised by a central authority. Just like our accounting profession, its people have looked to rules as a protection against criticism. If the rules are specific enough and I follow them carefully, I can't be faulted. Note that such a point of view is not so much interested in what is right and best in the specific situation as in self-protection in all situations. What we are doing here is a small thing in the big picture, but let's strike a blow for freedom of thought and innovation when we can, even if it is only a small one.

"The absence of profits and of any investor interest in them does mean that one of the major causes of litigation involving accountants is absent. Of course there will always be those who think the auditors have not done all they should in reviewing financial statements, but such litigation is more likely to be of the "breach of contract type" rather than the horrendous class action suits for alleged failure to comply with generally accepted auditing standards. Certainly the potential for legal action decreases when profits and the investor interest are removed. This country does not yet have the current litigious business environment we have in our country where everyone sues anyone at any possible opportunity. Finally, there is little if any need in nonprofit organizations to keep financial information confidential for competitive advantage purposes. So I recommend that we opt for general principles rather than rules and that we offer every legitimate encouragement to variety and innovation. This seems to me to be especially desirable when we think of the great variety that exists within not-for-profit organizations."

Some Early Conclusions

Not long after the above reported conversations, the team captain felt it might be well to articulate some of the conclusions the team had apparently reached. The process of doing so raised a number of points not specifically addressed in the preceding description of the team's deliberations, yet all seemed to follow logically from these discussions. Stated briefly, their recommendations ran as follows:

PRELIMINARY CONCLUSIONS

1. The focus of reporting should be on the basic questions in the minds of the general reader:

   a. What did the organization receive and from what sources?

   b. What did the organization do with what it received?

   c. How much does the organization have left?

   d. What are its plans for the future?

2. Because nonprofit organizations vary greatly in purpose and activity, freedom for innovation and for responsiveness to differences is essential.

3. Financial statement formats should not mimic those of business organizations. They should be adapted to the activities of the organization and should focus on answers to the questions above.

   a. Because equity is a concept not found in nonprofits, and because "fund balance" is not a meaningful term, a statement of net assets should replace the conventional (forprofit) balance sheet.

4. Business activities and not-for-profit activities by the same entity should be clearly distinguished for independent evaluation, and so their relative importance is apparent.

5. Assets and service facilities should be clearly distinguished.

   a. Service facilities should be reported separately from net assets. This should be a stewardship report accounting to readers for the care and keeping of all service facilities.

   Service facilities may be reported at historical cost, on a depreciated basis, or at an approximation of current value. The main purpose of this report is stewardship or accountability. Hence a general description of the extent, condition, and plans for these properties will be more informative than numbers alone. Depreciation calculations and disclosures are not required for income determination purposes, of course, and probably have little usefulness to anyone.

6. Commitments for a period of years into the future should be fully disclosed, properly classified as to probability and managment's priorities, and accompanied by sufficient explanation for the anticipated average reader.

7. Information relevant to the viability of management's plans for meeting commitments should be presented in conjunction with reported commitments. This information should include a record of receipts and their sources over a number of recent periods.

8. Fund distinctions should not be permitted to dominate the basic financial statements although the non-fungibility problem should be disclosed. Information on a fund basis may be disclosed in supplementary schedules if desired.

9. A management discussion and analysis of current and planned activities should be included. This could properly include relevant information about fund restrictions including either (1) an assertion that all such restrictions had been complied with appropriately or (2) a specification of any infringements accompanied by a description of planned remedies. Management's analysis should also include a thorough discussion of management's expectations and priorities, thereby adding useful and essential clarification to the summary of commitments.

Reporting Future Data

But the team captain's tentative conclusions did not escape without criticism. One of the team members felt very strongly about the implications in the captain's emphasis on future plans and commitments.

"It seems to me that when you call for the presentation of financial information about the future--things like plans and commitments--you have introduced a whole new element into our proposals. Our other recommendations have to do with some reclassifications and reinterpretations and the reduction of detail, but essentially we are working with the same historical data accountants have always dealt with. Now you suddenly suggest that we should require these people to present information about the future. Just how far into the future can any management predict what they will be able to do? And what will happen to them when they can't? Don't forget President Bush's "No new taxes!" And what are the implications for forprofit accounting? If nonprofits can provide reliable data about the future, why can't forprofits?"

The team captain had no opportunity to respond. Too many others wanted to voice their thoughts, some arguing for future data and some arguing against. Out of the ensuing discussion came at least the beginnings of a consensus.

First, forprofit organizations face a highly competitive environment. They obtain and hold customers on the basis of product quality, customer service, and price. How they beat the competition on any one of these factors may be information to be held confidential at all costs. Plans for the future, plans to do better than the competition in one or more of these factors, must be kept confidential if they are to succeed. Rarely do nonprofits face the same kind and extent of competion faced by forprofits.

Second, many nonprofit commitments are determinable with considerable accuracy; others are not. Careful classification and adequate disclosure is an essential, but nonprofits can experiment with the presentation of future information with relatively little serious financial risk. Finally, managerial accountability for nonprofits is a very difficult quality to obtain under present standards of reporting. Requiring the preparation and disclosure of budget type information would provide contributors and taxpayers information they could use in judging whether nonprofit management had lived up to its stated intentions. Such information would thus help in determining whether to take political action on the one hand or refuse contributions on the other. Most of the team agreed that requiring future data in financial statements was indeed departing from traditional accounting. At the same time, they found nonprofits so different from the forprofits for which traditional accounting had been developed that departures should be expected. The thought that they might--just might--bring a little accountability into the political process was a very real attraction.

One member, half in jest and half serious, summarized the feelings of all when he asked: "Can you imagine a presidential campaign in which the candidates presented their proposed budgets, even in general terms, and how they expected to finance them? What a difference from the sweeping generalities we get now!"

NOTES

1. This point is argued at length in "Financial Reporting: Should Government Emulate Business," Robert K. Mautz, *Journal of Accountancy*, August, 1989.

2. Few specifics emphasize the differences between forprofits and nonprofits more vividly than the nonprofit's need for properties that a forprofit would find most distasteful.

3. "Why Not-for-Profits Should Report Their Commitments," Robert K. Mautz, *Journal of Accountancy*, June, 1990.

CHAPTER 4
SOME PRO-FORMA
FINANCIAL REPORTING
FOR NONPROFIT ENTITIES

Bright and early the next morning, the team leader called his people together for a discussion of how to proceed with their assignment. Some of the team members were all ready to pack their bags and head for home. But the team leader had quite a different idea. His suggestion ran like this.

"Like most of you, I think we have discussed all the major issues that we can think of with respect to accounting and reporting by not-for-profit organizations. On a theoretical basis, we could certainly put together a set of defensible propositions for our client. But that does not mean we have finished our assignment. There is a big difference between resolving theoretical questions and finding a practicable solution to a real world problem. Some problems are not susceptible to neat, theoretical solutions. What we need to do now, is to put some of our ideas to the test. How would you like to prepare a set of financial statements for a real, live, not-for-profit organization?

"This won't be quite the same as completing a set of financial statements for a client, but it will be close enough to serve our purpose. Here is what I have in mind. We will break our team into three groups, each of which will serve as a mini-team for the purpose of this exercise. Remember the three entities whose financial statements we reviewed the other day? We will draw straws so that each team gets one of these. Then, using the data in those statements, prepare what you think would be the most informative set of financial statements for that organization.

"Make your pro forma statements tie in to the amounts given insofar as you can. If you need information that is not found in those statements, don't hesitate to make it up. Just keep any amounts you invent in reasonable range of those that are given. This will likely take a little longer than you anticipate, so we will give you until noon tomorrow to finish. Put your proposed financial statements in the best form you can. Bring them to me as soon as you are satisfied with them. I will have some transparencies made so we can use the overhead projector. Then right after lunch tomorrow we will have presentations and critiques, all strictly informal, of course.

"My hope, and expectation, is that this little exercise will force each of us to think about these theoretical issues in a very practical way. What will our conclusions look like in practice? Will they provide the kind of information someone can use to make the kinds of decisions we have talked about? Can we make the complex activities of these organizations actually understandable? Will the statements appeal to readers as helpful or will readers find them so formidable they never get past the first page? Now remember this is not a contest. Speed is not important. Take your time and do the best you can. Communication between teams is permitted, but we will all learn more if you see your specific assignment as different enough from the others to require a solution all its own."

Without listening to the groans and complaints from team members, the captain produced three straws, denominated the shortest as the State of Utah, the longest as the AARP, and, the mid-length straw as the AAA. Needless to say, the team that drew the short straw protested. Also, needless to say, the captain ignored all protests. In a remarkably short time, the three teams had each found space where its members could work together in reasonable peace and comfort, and had started drafting possible financial statements.

We need not follow them through their sometimes intensive discussions of how to tackle the assignment and then carry it to completion. Each team found some efforts unsuccessful. "Trial and error" best describes the process. A number of leads were abandoned; others were modified even after team members had agreed they were final. Later ideas caused modifications of early conclusions. By the end of the first day, there had been more than minor communication among the groups, but there were also comments such as: "Well, that's not a bad idea, but it sure doesn't work for our organization."

After an extension of half a day for the State of Utah team--an extension used for revisions and improvements by the other teams as well--the following pro forma financial statements for each of the organizations were presented. Preceding each set of statements is the essence of an oral summary by the team representative explaining why his team had selected the solution presented.

THE AMERICAN ACCOUNTING ASSOCIATION

Team Representative's Summary
The American Accounting Association presents a near-perfect case study for this kind of exercise. Its activities provide just enough variation to let us see how fund accounting might really confuse a reader if the organization were more complex, but they are still straightforward

enough that we can try different things without too big an investment of time. Although the AAA is an organization of accountants, one almost concludes that no one ever took an accountant's close look at its financial statements.

For example, what kind of an idea is "Current portion of deferred support" supposed to convey? It's not hard to think of more than one meaning for that particular combination of words. Certainly, part of the difficulty we had in putting these figures into pro forma statements was trying to interpret the language used in the formal financial statements.

Applying the theory of nonprofit financial reporting as we have developed it on this project, we found the published financial statements uninformative almost to the point of confusing. For example, we found little association of related expenditures and receipts, no apparent separation of forprofit and nonprofit activities, no recognition that cash-consumers and cash-producers should not be included in the same total, balance sheets with "fund balances," and no real basis for anticipating the future direction of the organization. Because the AAA is not at all complicated, you can see from our pro forma statements what we did about each of these matters.

Most of our conclusions fell right into place, but we did have a little discussion on how we might give a reader some idea of the financial condition of our nonprofit, taking plans for the future into account. One member of the team argued that because nonprofits are not involved in competitive activities, there is no reason why plans for some years into the future should not be presented. Thus if some change in activities were planned or a new emphasis scheduled that would call for additional amounts of resources, these could be set out and explained. The reader would then have a basis for considering whether he wants to support that change in emphasis or vote for a different slate of officers.

It took a little arguing for him to convince the other two members that what we referred to as "just a budget" should be viewed as a financial statement. But when we drafted one up, we found it contained some useful information and so we included it. Incidentally, I'm glad we were the first to be called on. The other teams heard us discussing this. We did get a little excited about it, so they sent their spies over to listen in. We don't know whether they accepted our idea or not, but if they did "You heard it here first."

The big thing about a budget (we called ours a statement of commitments) is that it calls for considerable management input. No one else knows what management has in mind. Not being members of this Association's executive committee, we had to make some assumptions in order to get a statement with a little something interesting to report. So we assumed a little growth in membership plus some inflation as probable increases over the next five years. Then, because of the widespread criticism of education and ethical standards generally, we anticipated the introduction of some special seminars on teaching improvements, legal hazards in accounting practice, and business ethics. We couldn't think of much else for new programs.

And one more thing. As you can see, we included the Association's liabilities at August 31, 1991, $210,000, as commitments to be met in the following year when they must be paid. Actually, there will be some liabilities carried over every year, the difference between "expenses" and "expenditures." For financial planning purposes, cash expenditures seemed to us more important than recording accruals to get expenses in the right years, so in effect we are shifting from an accrual to a cash basis in the 1991-92 fiscal year. Also, once we recognize that service facilities are different from assets, depreciation calculations for service facilities have little informative usefulness. Each year should bear the cash expenditure for service facilities acquired that year.

Proposed Financial Statements for the American Accounting Association

The following pro forma schedules were then projected and discussed.

AMERICAN ACCOUNTING ASSOCIATION
Pro Forma Statement of Service Facilities
at August 31, 1991 and 1990

	August 31 1991	August 31 1990
Land	$ 29,748	$ 29,748
Land improvements	15,252	15,252
Building	173,271	173,271
Furniture and equipment	113,295	107,600
Total, at cost	331,566	325,871
Less accumulated depreciation	197,868	176,669
Net of depreciation	$133,698	$149,202

All service facilities are:
    Fully used in the Association's activities.
    Unemcumbered by debt.
    Well maintained and serviced.
    Insured against normal business hazzards.

Except for minor replacements, they appear
adequate to meet the Association's needs for at
least the next ten years.

AMERICAN ACCOUNTING ASSOCIATION
Pro Forma Statement of Net Assets
at August 31, 1990 and 1991

ASSETS	1991	1990
Current Assets:		
Cash and cash equivalents	$1,098,625	$ 521,914
Investments	400,000	400,000
Current portion of pledges receivable	292,750	345,442
Accounts and interest receivable	115,740	46,984
Publications inventory	34,489	36,782
Prepaids (sic) and other assets	41,339	4,562
Total current assets	$1,982,943	$1,355,684
Other Assets:		
Pledges receivable, less current portion	$ 209,565	$ 301,818
Restricted assets, deferred compensation plan	167,471	88,500
Total other assets	$ 377,036	$ 390,318
Total assets	$2,359,979	$1,746,002

LIABILITIES

Current Liabilities:		
Accounts payable and accrued liabilities	$ 206,916	$ 211,317
Current portion of deferred revenue	375,094	316,686
Current portion of deferred support	630,547	250,734
Total current liabilities	$1,212,557	$ 778,737
Other Liabilities:		
Deferred compensation	$ 167,471	$ 88,500
Deferred revenue, less current portion	2,712	17,616
Deferred support, less current portion	148,965	306,865
Total other liabilities	$ 319,148	$ 413,081
Total liabilities	$1,531,705	$1,191,818
NET ASSETS	$ 828,274	$ 554,184

AMERICAN ACCOUNTING ASSOCIATION
Pro Forma Statement of Support and Expenditures
for the Years Ended August 31, 1991 and 1990

	Years ended August 31	
	1991	1990
Support from:		
Contributions	$1,269,059	$ 907,015
Membership dues	673,115	516,436
Annual convention:		
Revenues	$ 531,352	$420,463
Expenses	441,151	329,639
Interest and dividends	90,201	90,824
	55,221	49,032
Total Support	$2,087,596	$1,563,307

Uses of support:					
Programs and seminars:					
Costs	$1,303,393		$848,298		
Less contributions by participants	507,860	795,533		444,390	$ 403,908
Administration		666,069			835,015
Other expenses		223,859			29,868
Publications:					
Costs	$ 568,145		$637,940		
Less sales, subscriptions and advertising	551,781	16,364		430.900	207,040
Committees		55,813			48,946
Officers' meetings		48,749			44,756
Contribution to Financial Accounting Foundation		12,623			12,089
Fellowship grants		10,000			40,000
Total Uses of Support		$1,829,010			$1,621,622
Increase (decrease) in net assets		$ 258,586			$ (58,315)
Proportion of increase in assets obtained from nonprofit sources		93.0%			90.4%
Proportion of current year receipts expended		87.6%			103.7%

AMERICAN ACCOUNTING ASSOCIATION
Pro Forma Statement of Commitments
at September 1, 1991

	1991-92	1992-93	1993-94	1994-95	1995-96
For payment of present obligations	$ 210,000				
For continuation of programs:					
Administration	675,000	$ 680,000	$ 690,000	$ 700,000	$ 710,000
Programs and seminars	1,400,000	1,450,000	1,500,000	1,250,000	1,000,000
Publications	570,000	460,000	365,000	370,000	372,000
Officers' meetings	55,000	50,000	52,000	54,000	56,000
Committees	60,000	63,000	65,000	68,000	70,000
Fellowship grants	20,000	20,000	25,000	25,000	30,000
Contributions to Fin. Acctg. Foundation	15,000	15,000	17,000	17,000	18,000
Other programs	48,000	50,000	50,000	50,000	50,000
For new programs:					
Teaching improvement seminars		50,000	50,000		
Grants for new course development		20,000	20,000		
Total commitments	$3,053,000	$2,858,000	$2,834,000	$2,534,000	$2,306,000

Anticipated sources of support:					
Contributions, including existing pledges	$1,500,000	$1,000,000	$ 800,000	$ 750,000	$ 750,000
Membership dues	700,000	682,000	690,000	800,000	790,000
Annual convention	90,000	90,000	85,000	95,000	98,000
Seminar fees	725,000	800,000	800,000	720,000	650,000
Interest and dividends	50,000	50,000	50,000	50,000	50,000
Total anticipated support	$3,065,000	$2,622,000	$2,425,000	$2,415,000	$2,338,000
Anticipated annual excess (shortage)	$ 12,000	$ (236,000)	$ (409,000)	$ (119,000)	$ 32,000

During the team's discussion of the AAA pro forma financial statements, a number of interesting questions were raised. Although comments were generally complimentary of what was presented, the question of whether it was all worth while came up several times. If the membership is satisfied with the present statements--and they apparently are because the format didn't change over two years--is there any reason to think anyone reads them with any real interest? So why require changes? Another member noted that the AAA was a small organization with not very complicated activities. As a result, he suggested, anyone interested enough to give the statements a little time could understand the year's activities and results no matter how the data were presented. All that was needed was adequate disclosure.

Not all the members were sympathetic with both or either of these points of view as related to the AAA, but when the question was extended to other relatively simple nonprofits, the benefits of imposing accounting and reporting requirements different from generally accepted accounting principles were questioned. As one member put it: "Theory is great in its place, but unless the benefits are greater than the costs, why make changes?"

THE AMERICAN ASSOCIATION OF RETIRED PERSONS

Team Representative's Summary
To begin with, we couldn't decide whether our organization was a forprofit or a nonprofit. If there ever is a contest for the most profitable not-for-profit organization, we nominate the AARP for consideration. It certainly is engaged in some major profit-directed activities.

Although terms like "fund balance" are used, there is very little emphasis on conventional fund accounting or fund reporting. So we had difficulty convincing ourselves that the AARP does not already have financial statements appropriate to its activities. Because it does not now separate forprofit and nonprofit activities in its operating statement, we tried to do that. We also tried to obtain some more meaningful associations of expenses and receipts. We took some real liberties with the AARP figures in doing so.

For example, we didn't know what to do with the matching amounts of $79,645,000 for "Government grant revenues" and "Government grant expenses." The footnotes tell us that billings to the government include "the value of time spent by the grant host agency site supervisors and certain facility and supplies costs." The footnotes do not tell us how to separate charges for services rendered from facility and supply costs. Lacking that information, we left that activity out of our statements. The AARP footnotes state: "Such services and costs amounted to $8,252,000 and $6,613,000 in 1991 and 1990, respectively." We didn't think omission of these amounts would distort our statements unduly.

We give the AAA team full credit for its ideas about a statement of commitments, although we would certainly have come to the same conclusions sooner or later. We also made some unspecified assumptions about growth and inflation in plugging in expense figures. To add some new program expenditures, we decided that sooner or later the AARP will probably get into retirement communities and long-term care centers for its members. However, we also believe its astute management will move into these first on an experimental basis, rather than committing any great amount of resources.

Like the AAA team, we think there is something useful in reporting on the future plans of not-for-profit entities. In the absence of the profit motive and any equity interest, fear of litigation should not be a deterrent. We discussed the probable difficulty management would face in developing the necessary financial plans five years into the future. Obviously, the farther ahead one looks, the less clear the prospect. We finally agreed that a disclaimer should be added to that statement emphasizing that amounts for more than a year into the future were offered only as indications of direction with no assurance of their reliability whatever. As soon as we get back to the office, we will get our house counsel working on an appropriate wording. But we did feel that readers were entitled to some indication of where the Association was headed.

Proposed Financial Statements for the American Association of Retired Persons

AMERICAN ASSOCIATION OF RETIRED PERSONS
Pro Forma Statement of Net Assets (in thousands)
at December 31, 1991 and 1992

	December 31	
ASSETS	1991	1992
Cash	$ 2,692	$ 2,080
Treasury bills and notes	104,894	120,720
Short-term investments committed to unearned membership dues	125,526	$122,666
Accounts and notes receivable, net of allowances of $1,944 and $17,244	31,336	28,636
Prepaid expenses	8,856	8,961
Total assets	$273,304	$283,063

LIABILITIES

Unearned membership dues	$125,526	$122,666
Accounts payable	25,097	27,533
Accrued expenses	8,109	6,624
Accrued post-retirement health benefits	38,396	28,335
Total liabilities	$197,128	$185,158
NET ASSETS	$ 76,176	$ 97,905

The net asset amount does not include cash and
accounts receivable in the amount of $4,675 in
1991 and $4,480 in 1990 held under government
commitments and restricted to government grant
purposes.

AMERICAN ASSOCIATION OF RETIRED PERSONS
Pro Forma Statement of Receipts and Expenditures (in thousands)
for the years ended December 31, 1991 and 1990

	Years ended December 31	
NOT-FOR-PROFIT ACTIVITIES	1991	1990
Cost of member services:		
Publications	$105,012	$100,674
Less advertising revenues	41,105	42,751
	$ 63,907	$ 57,923
Programs and field services	61,011	56,973
Legislation, research, and development	22,356	18,607
Member services	51,835	46,980
Allocated share of administration and headquarters operation costs	22,973	17,750
Net increase in service facilities	12,228	10,354
Total cost of member services	$234,310	$208,587
Less members' dues, net:		
Total members' dues	$100,148	$101,935
Less cost of membership solicitation	7,791	13,725
	92,357	88,210
Net cost of member services	$141,953	$120,377

FOR-PROFIT ACTIVITIES

Revenues:		
Group insurance administrative allowances, net	$ 81,854	$ 75,165
Income from other programs and royalties	30.259	27,513
Interest income	43,588	47,960
Other income	454	532
Total	$156,155	$151,170
Less allocated share of administration and headquarters operation cost	35,931	26,626
Increase (decrease) in net assets from for-profit activities	120,224	124,544
Operating results, increase (decrease) in net assets	$(21,729)	$ 4,167
Proportion of net proceeds from profit-directed activities to total increases in net assets	56.6%	58.5%
Percent of current year's receipts expended for members' services	118.1%	96.6%

AMERICAN ASSOCIATION OF RETIRED PERSONS
Pro Forma Summary of Commitments (in thousands)
at December 31, 1991

	1992	1993	1994	1995	1996
Payments and/or funding of post-retirement benefits	$ 11,000	$ 11,000	$ 12,000	$ 12,000	$ 14,000
Continuing programs:					
Publications	60,000	60,000	60,000	60,000	60,000
Programs and field services	58,000	58,000	58,000	58,000	55,000
Legislation, research, and development	20,000	18,000	18,000	15,000	15,000
Member services and acquisition	60,000	60,000	60,000	60,000	60,000
Activities and facilities administration	30,000	35,000	35,000	38,000	38,000
Headquarters operation	19,000	22,000	22,000	22,000	23,000

New programs:					
Development of retirement communities for moderate income members		4,000	6,000	6,000	6,000
Development of long-term care centers		4,000	4,000	4,000	4,000
Acquisition of service facilities	2,500	1,000			
Total anticipated expenditures	$260,500	$273,000	$275,000	$275,000	$265,000
Anticipated sources of funds:					
For-profit activities	$140,000	$145,000	$150,000	$150,000	$150,000
Membership dues	105,000	108,000	110,000	115,000	118,000
Member "investments" in living and care facilities		5,000	8,000	12,000	
Use of present net assets	15,500		10,000		
Long-term debt		15,000		2,000	
Total anticipated receipts	$260,500	$273,000	$278,000	$279,000	$268,000

AMERICAN ASSOCIATION OF RETIRED PERSONS
Pro Forma Summary of Service Facilities
at December 31, 1991 and 1990

(In Thousands)

	December 31	
	1991	1990
Furniture and equipment	$34,684	$28,829
Leasehold improvements	11,787	9,414
Computer software	8,658	7,423
Total	$55,129	$45,666
Less accumulated depreciation and amortization	16,655	19,420
Net service facilities	$38,474	$26,246

General discussion of the AARP pro forma statements agreed that segregation of forprofit from nonprofit activities was desirable. Indeed, some members of the team were astounded to see that an organization officially recognized as nonprofit could be so extensively engaged in forprofit activities.

Another member went farther. He suggested that the AARP was a convincing example of an entity that should use both generally accepted accounting principles *for forprofit entities* and generally accepted accounting principles *for nonprofit entities*, each where applicable. Only by so doing, he argued, could a truly fair presentation result. Humorously, another member raised the question of whether that could subject the AARP to two different standard-setting bodies? To his surprise, there was general agreement that if there were to be a standard-setting body for forprofits and another for nonprofits, then the AARP should be subject to the requirements of both.

THE STATE OF UTAH

Team Representative's Summary

What an assignment! We have been wrestling with the 54 funds and two "account groups" specifically mentioned in our organization's 'Comprehensive Annual Financial Report' until our eyes are crossed. Frankly, we are more than a little unhappy. The State of Utah receives a 'Certificate of Merit' for the quality of its financial reporting. So this report must represent the best current financial reporting by state governments. If so, we don't know who is supposed to use such reports. There are some competent accountants on our mini-team, but we are overwhelmed by the quantity of detail, critical of the varying combinations of funds that make relating one statement to another a continuing puzzle, and baffled by the real purpose of such reporting.

I'm sure we've made some serious mistakes in preparing our pro forma statements. Time wasn't our real problem; what we needed was a guide. Many times we wished we could talk to those who put the original statements together.

Now that I have that off my mind, let me try to deal with our subject more objectively.

Like the AAA team, we found the combination of fund accounting and generally accepted accounting principles, as adapted to government reporting, totally unconcerned with the ideas we have been discussing in connection with this project. These financial statements also impressed us as not much concerned with their understandability to the average taxpayer. A great amount of information is presented, but it is presented in such a way as to discourage rather than encourage readers. If anyone responsible has given thought to the nature of this report's anticipated readership and the interests of that readership, that responsible party must have arrived at entirely different conclusions than we did. We would be very interested in the rationale that brought them to this form of reporting.

So, like the other mini-teams, we have tried to bring together into an understandable, overall report, a summary directed to those to whom the State's report is at least nominally addressed. We ignore the fractionalization into funds as distracting rather than enlightening. Granted, there may be some readers who are very interested in the financial condition of specific funds. Certainly, they are not the majority of those who should read these statements.

Management, of course, must be interested in every fund. To the extent management and others with special interests want this information, supporting schedules for such funds can be provided. We recognize also, that we have ignored the important point of the non-fungible nature of cash and some of the other assets. But this could readily be cared for with an explanatory note.

To us, an overall, general purpose report has wide appeal and usefulness. It should be the basic public reporting document; details, if necessary, can follow. After reviewing the state's report much more carefully than we did earlier, we think a statement by the state's auditors to the effect that funds have been expended only for appropriate purposes is all the detailed fund information either necessary or interesting to most readers. Of course, if such an assertion does not survive audit, then an explanation of any improper expenditures should be made with an explanation of what is needed to correct the error and whether such a correction has been effected.

The more we thought about it, the stronger we felt that a statement of commitments like the AAA team proposed has special application to a governmental organization, so we developed one too. We are not confident that we know just how to classify the State's commitments. They seem to range all the way from unavoidable expenditures to optimistic hopes. Some are not at all well described. Yet they tell a reader more about a political candidate's real intentions than do all the glib generalizations we get from campaign assertions. We think if candidates for executive office, and political parties generally, had to prepare and publish proposed statements of financial plans much like a statement of commmitments, voters could vote far more intelligently. And then they would have something definite against which to measure performance.

This is not to say that preparing such a statement is a simple matter. But doing so might be a very useful lesson in government to the candidate for public office. Of course the reader would have to be warned that the best laid plans could go astray. We think most voters already know that. Yet if one of the high points of a national convention were the presentation of a proposed budget, even if presented in general terms, it would tell the voter far more than he gets now. For example, if the Federal Government had reported publicly and understandably on this basis every year, the voters of this country might not have tolerated the incredible deficits our children and grandchildren now face.

In trying to prepare such a statement for the State of Utah, we also saw some genuine political problems in such informative reporting. For example, this state has operated conservatively over the years. It not only has relatively little debt, it has managed to accumulate some investments. These contribute a not insignificant amount of income to the state each year. When one remembers the political pressure in favor of spending, it is not hard to conceive of some "cause" seeing this resource as a way to get its purpose accomplished without an accompanying increase in taxes. This might not be to the state's best interests.

Then the thought was expressed that either one believes in democracy or one doesn't. So we opted for clear and understandable disclosure. If the politicians can't make their case persuasively enough, the people will suffer. That's what happens now.

Our Statement of Commitments proposes nothing very radical. After all, the state is doing very well financially. Utah derives substantial income from tourism. So we proposed some additional attention to roads and infrastructure to make many of the less known scenic areas more available to more people. Like good politicians, we assumed that doing so would result in additional tax receipts, so to some extent such expenditures may be self-liquidating.

Incidentally, we did get one gift. In the Comprehensive Annual Report we found a Statement of Fixed Assets and Natural Resources that looked so much like a Statement of Service Facilities we could do little more than summarize it for our report. I don't like to admit this, but sometimes I get the idea those people are ahead of us. And then I count the funds one more time, consider how unenlightening the current statements really are, and feel a lot better about our proposals.

We are impressed by the descriptive information included in the AAA stewardship report on service facilities. Obviously, we could do nothing like that for the State of Utah. But someone in the state administration could, and the results might be some very interesting information for readers.

I know I'm running over my time, but one last word. When we began this assignment, we were not all that enthused about the focus the whole team had settled on for financial reporting by nonprofit entities. It seemed much too simple and couched in non-accounting terms. The more we worked with it, however, the more those simple little questions seemed to lead us to reporting the information that a contributor or a taxpayer should be asking. So we are now fully converted to an annual report that answers the questions:

> How much did you get and from what sources?
> What did you do with it?
> How much do you have left?
> What are your plans for the future?

We had some discussion of the order in which the schedules answering these questions should be presented in a report. One member thought that inasmuch as service is the purpose of the organization, the services provided during the year might be the matter of greatest interest and should be presented first. This is certainly a possibility but he couldn't convince the rest of us to go along.

What impressed us most is the extent of useful and understandable information provided by organizing our report around those questions.

As shown in our pro forma statements, a reader can readily find the ratio of current year expenditures to current year receipts, an important indicator of the organization's focus. With appropriate classification of expenditures, a reader can also determine the proportion of receipts actually utilized for the purposes stated in soliciting or taxing the contributors of those receipts.

Another important bit of information can be found by comparing net assets at the end of the year with the year's expenditures, or with next year's commitments, to discover how long the organization could continue its present activities if receipts were reduced or ceased completely. We're confident that as we experiment more with this kind of reporting, we will find other ratios and comparisons of equal interest.

The other members of our group primed me to complain that preparing a report like this for a complex organization is a horrendous task, and that next time we want the American Accounting Association and the AAA team can have the State of Utah. But one reason this was such a difficult task was because we had to work from a set of financial statements prepared on a predetermined basis. If we had the books and records themselves, and if they were prepared with this kind of reporting in mind, putting the statements together would certainly not be the same problem we faced.

Proposed Financial Statements for the State of Utah

STATE OF UTAH
Pro Forma Statement of Net Assets
as of June 30, 1991

(In thousands)

ASSETS

Cash and cash equivalents	$1,469,730
Investments	5,385,413
Receivables	2,033,851
Inventories, prepaid items, and deferred charges	79,728
Deferred compensation plan assets	120,171
Amount available in debt service fund	12,336
Total assets	$9,101,229

LIABILITIES

Vouchers, notes, and contracts payable	$ 279,339
Accrued liabilities and deferred revenues	241,754
Deposits, taxes, etc. due to others	1,022,190
Policy claim liabilities	383,863
General obligation bonds payable	239,295
Revenue bonds payable	1,675,309
Leave and deferred compensation liabilities	168,456
Total liabilities	$4,010,206
NET ASSETS	$5,091,023

THE STATE OF UTAH
Pro Forma Statement of Increase in Net assets
for the Year Ended June 30, 1991
(in thousands)

INCREASES IN ASSETS
Taxes:

Sales	$ 744,764
Individual income	717,616
Motor and special fuel	167,842
Corporate taxes	91,451
Miscellaneous fines, etc.	127,939
Federal grants and contracts	854,904
Premiums, licenses, permits, fees, and departmental collections	280,506
Miscellaneous receipts and aeronautics	61,261
Total taxes	$3,046,283

Contributions by pension plan members	$ 199,183
Proceeds of revenue bonds/ contracts	10,100
Proceeds of general obligation bonds	20,139
Operating transfers in	188,402
Residual equity transfers	1,169
Total	$ 418,993

Net income from profit-directed activities:	
Interest on investments	$ 303,335
Internal service funds	22,348
Enterprise funds	19,659
Total from profit-directed activities	$ 345,342
Total increases in assets	$3,810,618

```
        DECREASES IN ASSETS
Costs of:
  General government                  $   209,550
  Human services                          415,873
  Corrections                              77,695
  Health                                  415,359
  Higher education                        312,796
  Natural resources                        68,129
  Business, labor, and agri-
    culture                                28,020
  Community and economic
    development                            63,547
  Unemployment claims                      72,541
  Public education                        980,634
  Transportation and public
    safety                                382,224
  Miscellaneous                             3,709
      Total government services       $3,030,077

Interest and other debt service
  charges                             $    17,331
Debt principal retirement                  46,790
      Total debt service              $    64,121

Capital outlay                        $    80,450
Pension benefits claimed                  147,839
Operating transfers out                   171,544
Residual equity transfers                   2,990
      Total                           $   402,823

      Total decreases in assets       $3,497,021

      NET INCREASE IN ASSETS          $   313,597
```

STATE OF UTAH
Pro Forma Summary of Commitments (in thousands)
at June 30, 1991

	Years Ended				
	6-30-92	6-30-93	6-30-94	6-30-95	6-30-96
Payment of long-term debt	$ 37,965	$ 70,855	$ 58,475	$ 52,000	$ 20,000
Interest on debt	17,000	17,000	15,000	14,000	17,000
Continuation of programs:					
General government	210,000	215,000	215,000	221,000	223,000
Public safety	52,000	52,000	54,000	54,000	57,000
Human services	482,000	490,000	498,000	498,000	510,000
Corrections	82,000	85,000	115,000	95,000	98,000
Health	440,000	448,000	450,000	455,000	455,000
Higher education	410,000	410,000	500,000	530,000	535,000
Natural resources	70,000	70,000	73,000	73,000	75,000
Business, labor, and agriculture	30,000	30,000	32,000	32,000	33,000
Community and economic development	66,000	72,000	72,000	75,000	75,000
Public education	1,000,000	1,050,000	1,050,000	1,100,000	1,100,000
Transportation	335,000	400,000	400,000	400,000	400,000
Unemployment claims	72,000	70,000	65,000	65,000	65,000
New programs:					
None planned					
Total commitments	$3,303,965	$3,479,855	$3,597,475	$3,664,000	$3,663,000

Anticipated sources of financing:					
Present taxes at current rates and increased economic activity	$1,840,000	$1,860,000	$1,900,000	$1,900,000	$1,950,000
Federal grants and contracts	865,000	860,000	850,000	850,000	850,000
Other state activities	915,000	930,000	940,000	950,000	960,000
New long-term debt			100,000	100,000	
Total anticipated receipts	$3,620,000	$3,650,000	$3,790,000	$3,800,000	$3,760,000

STATE OF UTAH

Pro Forma Summary of Service Facilities and Natural Resources (in thousands)

at June 30, 1991

	Land	Buildings and Im-provements	Equipment	Total
General government	$11,246	$112,988	$ 26,597	$150,831
Business, labor, and agriculture	172	5,241	4,410	9,823
Natural resources	50,149	48,136	12,160	110,445
Higher education			617	617
Public education	1,887	44,723	20,235	66,845
Human services	2,906	57,951	17,274	78,131
Corrections	683	82,799	7,537	91,019
Health	51	3,597	12,920	16,568
Public safety	3,481	23,387	18,136	45,004
Transportation	14,209	46,282	76,682	137,173
Community development	85	10,873	6,469	17,427
Total service facilities and natural resources	$84,869	$435,977	$203,037	$723,883
Construction in progress				81,359
Total service facilities, completed and in progress, and natural resources				$805,242

CHAPTER 5
SOME CONCLUSIONS

Although none of the team members told the team leader they had enjoyed the experience, he was quietly pleased by the success of his exercise in practical reporting. Everyone was now much better acquainted with current reporting practices and with the very real problems involved. But before raising the idea of final conclusions, he wanted to test, one more time, their enthusiasm for the ideas they seemed agreed to. He began with this kind of a challenge.

"Under current accounting practice, there is really only one set of generally accepted accounting principles. The Financial Accounting Standards Board continues to study how best to apply these business accounting principles to not-for-profit organizations other than governments. We also have a Government Accounting Standards Board, and it is currently addressing the problems of financial accounting and reporting for governmental entities. But what you seem prepared to propose as the result of this assignment does not agree with either generally accepted accounting principles or the proposals of the Government Accounting Standards Board. Conventional accountants will view us as being way out in left field. Now it's true that our proposals are not directed at practice in the United States, but you know that sooner or later they will come to someone's attention and then we could be under considerable criticism.

Most American accountants with our assignment would draw heavily on U.S. practice. How would you respond to criticism that we failed to do so? Let me suggest four specific topics. If you think of any others, we can put them on the list also. Unless we are convinced that we have logical responses to any and all criticism on these items, perhaps we had better think again.

1. Accrual accounting--we haven't said a word about it.

2. Generally accepted accounting principles--some of our proposals will sound like heresy to most accountants.

3. Fund accounting--our proposals are to report as if there were no fund distinctions, but to many government officers and accountants, a financial transaction is not a transaction until the fund to which it relates is identified. Funds are the entities within which financial activities take place.

4. Budgeting--some accountants consider the budget as the primary control device for both governments and other nonprofit organizations. Without a profit figure to reveal how well management has succeeded, they feel comparisons of actual results with budgeted expectations should be required. Generally accepted accounting principles do not include this idea, of course, because they were developed primarily for business organizations. But governmental accountants are likely to think that we are not very forward looking if we do not call for publication of the budget at the beginning of the year and a comparison with actual results at the end.

"Now, who is ready to respond to one or more of these items? Or to add to the list, if you wish?"

Budget Comparisons with Actual

"Let me try that one about the budget. I don't know what our 'statement of commitments' is if it isn't a budget. Actually, we call for a multi-year budget. The nature of many nonprofit entity projects and programs is such that management must plan well beyond the current year. Our statement of commitments provides a long-term budget view of things. We show five years as an example. It can be as much longer as the readers demand.

"From the standpoint of contributors and taxpayers, the statement of commitments should be the one that draws the most interest. In that statement, management lays out its plans, at least on a tentative basis, years in advance. At the end of each year, our other schedules will permit comparisons of actual receipts and expenditures with that plan. This statement will then put nonprofit management under pressure to do some serious planning. Then when things don't work out as planned, management will have to explain in its next report what went wrong and why.

"I suppose someone could complain that our statement of commitments does not provide enough information about the receipts side. Perhaps we should be sure to include a requirement that the planned financing of all commitments be disclosed fully.

"But I have to add one word more. I have never been exactly enthusiastic about evaluating performance on how well a man meets or beats his budget. After all, it is his budget. He knows more about it than anyone else. How difficult is it for him to build in a little slack so he can show he has been real economical and efficient in his operations? How difficult is it for him to defer a little maintenance if he is about to run over? I wouldn't have any great disagreement with requiring comparisons of actual and budget, but frankly, I wouldn't put a whole lot of faith in them myself.

"What I think would be more important would be a good, annual MD&A (management discussion and analysis) in which management accounted for its actions during the past year and its plans for the next. The managment could describe the tentative nature of some commitments, the inevitability of others, and the reasons why the budget might not be met exactly. With that kind of information and our proposed financial statements, even the average reader could make useful comparisons of plans and accomplishments. And I'm fully convinced that intimate participation by management in the preparation of not-for-profit entity financial statements is a must if they are to be at all useful."

Accrual Accounting

"The one about accrual accounting is made for me. My Dad served as mayor of our town for two terms. He got so mad at the CPAs who came in to audit the books, he tried to discourage me from taking accounting. If he had been sitting in on our discussions, he wouldn't have believed we could be so sensible.

"His big beef was accrual accounting. He couldn't see any sense in applying it to the town. And I couldn't see much sense to his unhappiness until our team began to look at the differences between forprofits and nonprofits. Accrual accounting is designed to get the most accurate measurement of income and financial position possible. It always looks for the substance of a transaction or event rather than its form. That's very good, but the fact is that nonprofit transactions are not aimed at income and so are generally of a different type than forprofit transactions. Forprofit expenses are designed to bring in revenue; nonprofit expenditures are not. Forprofit revenues come only because of expenses; most nonprofit receipts come 'free,' so to speak. If accrual accounting really means 'substance over form,' we are all for it. We just want those who tell us what substance is in nonprofit transactions to understand the real nature of those transactions.

"As my Dad pointed out, the two biggest accrual items, inventories and depreciation, are of little importance in city finances. He contended that cash transactions are the essence of municipal finance. Once money is paid out, it is gone forever. He also ran a small business so he knew what income measurement and financial position meant in a forprofit. He also knew there was a difference between running the town and running his business. Poor old guy just couldn't articulate that difference.

"I would add to his arguments that our financial statements, with a statement of commitments included, does through disclosure what good business accounting does with its concepts of capital maintenance and accrual. If nonprofit management prepares a good statement of commitments, and especially if it includes a good MD&A as just suggested, we have accomplished everything for nonprofit entities that conventional accrual accounting does for businesses. And we haven't restricted the nonprofit's reporting freedom with a lot of inappropriate requirements. What we have proposed is not that GAAP be abandoned for nonprofits. Not at all. GAAP should be applied where it fits--and only where it fits. We also need some generally accepted accounting principles for nonprofits that prescribe accounting and reporting for the rest of the nonprofit's activities."

A dissenting voice broke in sharply at this point. "Wait just a minute. I don't know how big a town you are speaking of, but you're giving accrual accounting a bum rap. Some people think accrual accounting is solely income oriented, but as you noted briefly in passing, it is indeed directed at getting at substance rather than only form. That should be just as important in not-for-profits as in business. Take the kinds of warranties and guarantees the government makes to insure bank accounts and deposits in thrift institutions and the like. Some of these present very complex questions about the nature and extent of the resulting obligations. If we are to classify commitments on any sensible basis, we will need lots of attention to both form and substance. Rather than dismissing substance over form so quickly, I would say we may need considerable research and study to determine how best to classify and report such items in the financial statements of nonprofits.

"Perhaps the most important point to make here is that accrual accounting as developed for business organizations has neglected important problems highly relevant to the financial condition of some nonprofit entities like the federal government. We can't begin to resolve these problems in this project, but let's not ignore their existence. If our ideas for financial reporting by not-for-profit entities are adopted, applying them will call for the development of some heretofore neglected accounting theory. The accrual concept should be the basis for that development."

Differences Among Not-for-Profits

The team leader found this a timely moment to make a general comment on the wide variety of organizations that fall within the not-for-profit classification and the need to recognize such differences in any statement of principles. This carried the team over what might otherwise have been a stressful confrontation. It also led to another question.

"May I ask whether this is all worth while? Or let me phrase that another way. Do we think that all nonprofits should be required to follow the same principles? Just contrast the three we have studied. They differ greatly. The American Accounting Association, like many other nonprofits, could present its financial statements in a number of ways and not really mislead anyone. The American Association of Retired Persons is certainly into business in a big way, so the identification and separation of its for-profit and not-for-profit activities is essential. The State of Utah has an entirely different kind of problem, one of great variety in its activities, and a mass of detail to present in an intelligible way. Neither the AAA nor Utah has any great need to separate profit-directed from nonprofit activities. I can see why large and/or complex nonprofits need reporting requirements, but how about all the little ones like condominium associations, local charities, and associations?"

This stirred up considerable discussion. Sensing that time was slipping away with no real progress, the team leader tried to bring the group back on track. "There is much in what you say. The variety within the nonprofit group requires careful consideration, but there may be a better solution than just exempting some of them from any reporting requirements at all. I think there are two closely related issues. First, how tightly should financial reporting for nonprofits be restricted? Second, what kind of restriction will serve best? Remember, we are engaged to provide expert advice. At this point, I think the best advice we can give runs something like this. No matter how small or uncomplicated a nonprofit may be, those who contribute to it have a right to know how their contributions are used. That is really all we are concerned with, financial reporting that gives those who contribute to nonprofits a fair reporting of what happened to their money and what is likely to happen to any additional contributions or taxes.

"As long as that reporting is both complete and understandable, need we ask for anything more? We have discussed before that those who read the general purpose financial statements of nonprofits have very different interests than do those who read the financial statements of forprofits. Those who read and rely on the financial statements of nonprofits will not have an interest in comparative net profit amounts. Of course they may make some comparisons among entities but not for the same purpose nor in the same way. Thus considerable flexibility can be permitted to nonprofit management in the way it presents its activities and the results of those activities.

"Freedom to experiment widely with financial statement formats because of peculiarities in their organizations or activities may pose no real threat to anyone. How they report may not be nearly as important as what they report. If our recommendations are in the form of principles to be observed rather than rules to be followed, we can provide flexibility with little likelihood that anyone would be misled. I think it would be a mistake for us to prescribe reporting formats. Let us formulate sound principles and then permit as much flexibility as possible as long as the principles are not violated. If we can agree on that kind of approach, differences in size and complexity become much less important. Do any of you have any difficulty in proceeding on that basis?

"Good. That seems to leave only fund accounting. Who wishes to deal with that subject?"

Fund Accounting and Fund Financial Reporting

"Perhaps it's because I was assigned to the State of Utah team that I have such strong feelings about fund accounting. But let me make myself clear: *fund accounting* and *fund financial reporting* are quite different things. If management finds fund accounting useful, by all means use it. But it's a fact of life that when you report on a fund basis, you confuse and lose your readers. General purpose financial statements should not be fractionated into funds. This does not mean that readers are not interested in whether management has observed the restrictions of endowment funds, special taxes, and the like. Of course they are interested; scrupulous observance of requirements is a must for anyone with a public trust.

"But that certainly does not call for fund reporting. A single statement by the management and attested to by the independent auditors would carry all the useful information that most readers can use. 'All restrictions imposed on the expenditure of funds by law or agreement have been observed during the period reported.' Of course if this were not true, management would have to say so and explain what it was doing to remedy the situation. We might also need to point out that the general financial statements are not intended to note all fund distinctions and requirements, so to that extent they are incomplete. But I don't know why we would need anything more in the general financial statements.

"Let me make my point another way. Consider for a moment what a report by one of the biggest Fortune 500 companies would look like if the company omitted financial statements for the entity as a whole and instead reported on each and every one of its 54 or more functions with a full set of funds-type financial statements. Certainly its competitors would be delighted and might well pore over every set of those statements. But what would the shareholders do? What could they make of such a display? The argument that funds in a government or other nonprofit are functional entities may well be true. Certainly it may justify fund accounting, and perhaps fund reporting, for management. But if the purpose of financial reporting is the communication of information, fund detail certainly has no place in public financial reporting.

"Wait a minute. Let me be a little cautious with that last statement. There may indeed be those who have a keen interest in a given fund or activity. We should say nothing in our report about restricting the extent of fund reporting. If the State of Utah had a good overall, general purpose report, I wouldn't care how many fund reports it produced in support as long as all of these could be tied in with the basic statements. But it seems to me, the first reporting responsibility should be to serve the citizens and taxpayers of the state. After that, other than the cost involved, there is no harm in serving the interests of those who need fund reporting also.

Rules and Procedures

A team member who had listened intently but said nothing during the preceding discussions now had a suggestion. "Before we leave this, it seems to me one of the questions we will certainly have to answer has to do with why we haven't specified any rules and procedures. Maybe I've been in accounting too long, but a page full of principles doesn't look like much of a report."

The only real old-timer on the team immediately raised his hand to respond. "Would you believe I can remember back when there wasn't either an FASB or a GASB? And Intermediate Accounting textbooks could be carried with one hand? In my opinion, all these rules and procedures that now constitute generally accepted accounting principles are the result of a very few factors: (1) a real decline in general professionalism, (2) too much competition for clients, and (3) the horrendous litigation situation that seems to engulf the general practice of accounting. The fact of the matter is we need rules and established procedures to protect ourselves from litigation. As long as we abide by the professional rules, we have a basis for protecting ourselves in court.

"But for nonprofits, as we have discussed a number of times, we anticipate relatively little litigation. We can once again act like professionals. That is, we can agree on basic principles, apply them in specific cases to the best of our ability, and not be threatened with the loss of everything we own every time we sign an audit opinion. Because profit dollars are not involved, managements will not be after us for the loosest possible interpretation of applicable rules. Competition within the profession will again be on the basis of quality of service, not on interpretation of rules. Not-for-profit accounting will remind some of us of the good old days. The short answer to your question, my friend, is that we don't propose rules and procedures for nonprofits because we don't need them. We have principles to guide us and that's all we need."

At this point, the man who had asked the question wished he hadn't, and his respondent's breath had run out.

Some General Principles for Financial Reporting by Nonprofit Entities

As no one suggested any additional criticism for discussion, the team leader thought now would be the time to direct attention to some possible conclusions for their engagement. While the rest of the team members had been working with one or another of the three cases, he had put together some "general principles" drawn from their study and discussion. These would serve as a starting point in working toward conclusions. He didn't think his proposal would long survive once the team members had it in hand, but he also knew he needed some way to focus their attention. He used the tentative conclusions at the end of Chapter 3 as a beginning.

The team captain was both right and wrong. The team members were very critical of some of his draft principles. Almost everyone likes to edit the work of others. But they had also participated in the same study and discussions he had so they tended to see many things the same way. Actually, their preceding discussions had been very useful to all of them. When these were combined with their recent "practical experiment" and the opportunity to meetlikely criticisms, his team members were more than ready to propose "principles." The following conclusions emerged.

Proposed Principles for Financial Reporting by Nonprofit Entities

A. Not-for-profit organizations are sufficiently different from business organizations that the generally accepted accounting principles developed for business entities cannot be expected to meet the needs of nonprofit entities without some modifications.

> 1. Nonprofit entities have no interest that compares with the present or potential equity interests in business entities.

> 2. Nonprofit entities do have interests faced with decisions, but these decisions call for a markedly different set of decision data than is required by the equity interests in business organizations.

B. The differences between for-profit and nonprofit entities in purpose, operations, measures of performance, use of resources, viability, relationships among interests, and relevant decision information call for specific differences in their accounting and financial reporting.

C. Financial reporting for nonprofit entities requires concepts ("service facilities" and "commitments") not found in present generally accepted accounting principles.

1. Service facilities are useful, desirable, and often costly properties that, when used in a nonprofit entity's activities, are cash-consuming rather than cash-generating.

a. Service facilities should be accounted for as the valuable properties they are, reported on a stewardship basis, and not included in totals with the entity's assets.

2. Commitments are intentions calling for financial expenditures that may or may not eventuate.

a. Commitments should be identified, classified as to relative priority and/or avoidability, and reported along with the entity's historical fund-raising record as essential information for estimating the entity's continuing viability.

D. The concepts of net income and owners' equity, important in business accounting and reporting, have no place in the accounting and reporting for nonprofit entities.

E. Some conventional reporting formats for business organizations may be inappropriate for many nonprofit entities.

F. Nonprofit organizations' financial reports are most useful to contributors and/or taxpayers if they focus on questions such as:

1. How much did the entity receive during the reporting period and from what sources?

2. What did the entity do with what it received?

3. How much does the entity have left?

4. What are the entity's plans and commitments for the future?

G. In the financial reports of nonprofit entities, sources of receipts from, and the extent of expenditures for, profit-directed activities should be clearly separated from receipts and disbursements related to not-for-profit activities.

H. Differences among entities within the not-for-profit category are almost as significant as the differences between for-profits and not-for-profits. Requiring all not-for-profit entities to report in compliance with a firm set of fixed rules and formats would not necessarily lead to the most informative reporting. Considerable flexibility in manner and style of display can be permitted as long as the conceptual differences noted in the forgoing requirements are observed.

Conclusion

Knowing his team members were eager to get home to their families, the team leader released all but one other member. Then the two of them settled down to draft their final report. They planned to tie it directly to their proposed principles, but knew they would have to support every conclusion with both explanation and illustrations. As they pulled the draft together, one or the other would now and then remember a specific contribution and how a given point came into the team's discussion. Neither of them had anticipated a report anything like the one they found themselves now developing, yet they agreed they were well satisfied.

Close to the end of their work, the team leader of the business accounting team dropped in to see how things were going. Curiously, he leafed through some of their draft material, read their tentative principles, and inquired about the size of their report. Finally he could restrain himself no longer.

"This sure beats me. Where are your quotations from Generally Accepted Accounting Principles? Surely you know the AICPA recommends GAAP for nonprofits. Where are your citations of authoritative literature? What do you guys think you are? Revolutionaries or something? I've never seen a report like this."

"Well John" was the only response he received, "You really need to read the full report. Probably more than once. All we did was 'take a fresh look.' That gave us a whole new perspective. You ought to try it some time."

ANNOTATED BIBLIOGRAPHY

1. *Financial Reporting by Not-for-Profit Organizations: Form and Content of Financial Statements.* Norwalk, CT: Financial Accounting Standards Board, 1989.

   An "invitation to comment" on a research project of the Financial Accounting Standards Board. Includes 23 issues, with sub-issues, considered relevant to possible future financial accounting standards. Includes *Display in the Financial Statements of Not-for-Profit Organizations,* prepared by the American Intitute of Certified Public Accountants Not-for-Profit Task Force, December 16, 1988. Report includes 26 pages of illustrative financial statements.

2. Mautz, R.K., "Financial Reporting: Should Government Emulate Business?" New York: *Journal of Accountancy,* 1981.

   An analysis of differences between the activities and properties of business corporations and state and local governments, and the implications such differences have for accounting and financial reporting. This leads to the conclusion that forcing state and local accounting and financial reporting into the business balance sheet and income statement models will fail to meet the nees of most of the interests to be served and will also strain the reporting model so drastically that the resulting figures will be of little use to anyone.

3. Mautz, R.K., "Monuments, Mistakes, and Opportunities," Sarasota, FL, *Accounting Horizons,* 1988.

   Contrasts the causes and results of cash flows in business organizations and in not-for-profit organizations and concludes that the latter do not have a causal relationship between expenditures and receipts as do business organizations. Some properties owned by not-for-profits are acquired and employed with the knowledge that, unlike assets, their use will create a net cash outflow over time rather than a net cash inflow. As such, they represent a concept unfamiliar to busines accounting. This leads to the thought that the accounting for such properties should not be the same as the accounting for properties that do meet the definition of an asset.

4. Mautz, R.K., "Not-for-Profit Financial Reporting: Another View," New York. *Journal of Accountancy*, 1989.

    Argues that "service facilities," valuable properties acquired by a not-for-profit organization with the intention and expectation that they will result in a net cash outflow over their lifetimes, do not meet the FASB definition of an asset and therefore require special accounting and financial reporting separate from the organization's properties that do meet the definition of an asset. Also suggests that the acquisition of service facilities in itself represents a commitment to continue supplying the service for which the facility was acquired, thereby having implications for the future much like a liability.

5. Mautz, R.K., "Why Not-for-Profits Should Report Their Commitments," New York. *Journal of Accountancy*, 1990.

    Points out the variety of commitments for future expenditure of resources that not-for-profits may incur, and notes that many do not meet the requirements of a liability and therefore are not reported in the organization's financial statements. Argues that generally accepted accounting principles for business organizations are inadequate to obtain appropriate disclosure of the financial condition of a not-for-profit entity.

6. Mautz, R.K., "Generally Accepted Accounting Principles and Federal Government Financial Reporting," Washington. *Public Budgeting & Finance*, 1991.

Presents a case against attempts to apply generally accepted accounting principles for business corporations to financial reporting for the federal government. Private business and the federal government are contrasted in the way decisions are made, the purpose of their activities, measures of their success, choices available to recipients of their services, nature of cash inflows, nature of basic interests, basic concepts for reporting purposes, confidentiality of management plans, the kinds of information most useful to interested parties. A list of issues in federal financial reporting requiring resolution is offered.

INDEX